# Further Physics

## David Sang

WITHDRAWN

Series editor
**Fred Webber**

**CAMBRIDGE**
UNIVERSITY PRESS

Published by the Press Syndicate of the University of Cambridge
The Pitt Building, Trumpington Street, Cambridge CB2 1RP
40 West 20th Street, New York, NY 10011-4211, USA
10 Stamford Road, Oakleigh, Melbourne 3166, Australia

First published 1996

Printed in Great Britain at the University Press, Cambridge

A catalogue record for this book is available from the British Library

ISBN 0 521 55606 6 paperback

Designed and produced by Gecko Ltd, Bicester, Oxon

This book is one of a series produced to support
individual modules within the Cambridge Modular
Sciences scheme. Teachers should note that written
examinations will be set on the content of each module
as defined in the syllabus. This book is the author's
interpretation of the module.

Front cover photograph: False-colour image showing the air flow
around a bullet moving at $500 \, \text{m s}^{-1}$. The image was recorded using
laser interferometry; Philippe Plailly/Science Photo Library

# Contents

# Acknowledgements

1, John Lawrence/Tony Stone Images; 6, Roger G Howard; 7, 9, NASA/Science Photo Library; 8, Dr Jeremy Burgess/Science Photo Library; 10, Worldsat International/Science Photo Library; 13, Jonathan Watts/Science Photo Library; 14, 15, 20*tl*, 20*tr*, 20*c*, 26, 36*t*, 36*b*, 39, 55, 56, 62, 65, 69, 71, Andrew Lambert; 19, Philippe Plailly/ Science Photo Library; 29, *La Fée Electricité* by Raoul Dufy (1937), from the Musée Nationale d'Art Moderne, Paris/The Bridgeman Art Library; 31, Michael Brooke; 35, Science Photo Library; 41, Dave Merron; 60, Manchester City Engineers; 61, 67, dp photographic/National Power plc; 64*t*, Prontaprint/The National Grid Company; 64*b*, Robin Scagell/Science Photo Library

# Circular motion

1 express angular displacement in radians;

2 understand and use the concept of *angular velocity*;

3 recall and use the equation for velocity:

   $v = r\omega$

4 recall and use the equation for centripetal acceleration:

   $a = r\omega^2$

5 recall and use the equation for centripetal force:

   $F = mr\omega^2$

## Angular displacement

For an object moving in a straight line, we can describe its motion in terms of its displacement $s$, velocity $v$ and acceleration $a$. If we are to give a full description of the motion (kinematics) of an object moving in a circle, we need to choose appropriate ways in which to do so. We could continue to use $s$, $v$ and $a$; however, these quantities are defined to make it easy to describe linear motion. For circular motion, it helps to define terms that are similar, but which reflect the fact that we are considering something which follows a circular path.

We are used to telling the time by looking at the hands of a clock *(figure 1.1)*. The positions of the hands are constantly changing as they move around the clockface, and we use their angular displacements to tell us the time. The meaning of angular displacement is shown in *figure 1.2*; it is the angle through which the object has moved from some fixed reference point. (On a clockface, this point is the 12 at the top.) We use the symbol $\theta$ (Greek letter theta) to represent this angle.

We know the precise position of the moving object if we know two quantities: its angular displacement $\theta$ and the radius of the circle $r$. As it moves, $\theta$ changes while $r$ remains constant. (We could also have defined its position in terms of two

● *Figure 1.1* Circular motion on the face of Big Ben.

coordinates $x$ and $y$, but this would give us awkward equations to handle later on, since both $x$ and $y$ change all the time.)

### SAQ 1.1

a By how many degrees does the angular displacement of the hour hand of a clock change each hour?

b Think about a clock which is showing 3.30. What are the angular displacements (in degrees) from the 12 at the top to the minute hand, and to the hour hand?

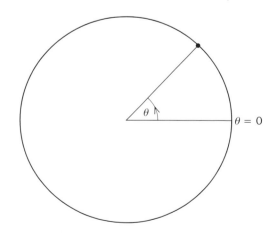

● *Figure 1.2* Defining angular displacement. Angles are conventionally measured anticlockwise as shown.

## Radians

In practice, it is usual to measure angles and angular displacements in units called radians rather than in degrees. One **radian** is defined such that there are $2\pi$ radians (rad) in a complete circle (*figure 1.3*). In other words:

$$2\pi\,\text{rad} = 360° \quad \text{and} \quad \pi\,\text{rad} = 180°$$

From this it follows that 1 rad is equal to $360°/2\pi$, so that:

$$1\,\text{rad} \approx 57.3°$$

If you can remember that there are $2\pi\,\text{rad}$ in a full circle, you will be able to convert between radians and degrees:

to convert from degrees to radians, multiply by $2\pi/360°$;

to convert from radians to degrees, multiply by $360°/2\pi$.

We shall now do an example. If $\theta = 60°$, what is the value of $\theta$ in radians?

Answer: $\theta = 60°$

$$= 60° \times \frac{2\pi}{360°}\,\text{rad}$$

$$= \frac{\pi}{3}\,\text{rad}$$

$$= 1.05\,\text{rad}$$

(Note that it is often useful to express an angle as a multiple of $\pi$ radians.)

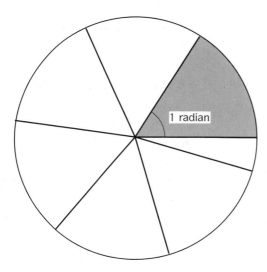

● **Figure 1.3** There are $2\pi$ radians in a complete circle.

## SAQ 1.2

a Convert the following angles from degrees into radians: 30°, 90°, 105°.

b Convert these angles from radians to degrees: 0.5 rad, 0.75 rad, $\pi$ rad, $\pi/2$ rad.

c Express the following angles as multiples of $\pi$ radians: 60°, 90°, 180°, 360°.

## Defining an angle

The definition of the radian comes from the way in which an angle is defined (*figure 1.4a*). If an object moves a distance $s$ around a circular path of radius $r$, its angular displacement $\theta$ is given by

$$\text{angle} = \frac{\text{length of arc}}{\text{radius}} \quad \text{or} \quad \theta = \frac{s}{r}$$

Since both $s$ and $r$ are distances measured in metres, it follows that the angle $\theta$ is simply a ratio. It is a dimensionless quantity. We give it units of radians. If the object moves twice as far around a circle of twice the radius (*figure 1.4b*), its angular displacement is the same:

$$\theta = \frac{2s}{2r} = \frac{s}{r}$$

If the object moves all the way round the circumference of the circle, it moves a distance $2\pi r$. Its angular displacement is then $2\pi r/r = 2\pi\,\text{rad}$. Hence a complete circle contains $2\pi\,\text{rad}$.

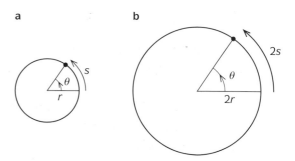

● **Figure 1.4** The size of an angle depends on the radius and the length of the arc. Doubling both leaves the angle unchanged.

## SAQ 1.3

A racing car travels 200 m around a circular track of radius 120 m. What is its angular displacement (in radians) from the starting line?

## SAQ 1.4

The Earth orbits the Sun at a distance of $150 \times 10^6$ km in approximately 365 days.

**a** What is its angular displacement (in radians) in 1 day?

**b** How far does it travel around its orbit in 1 day?

# Angular velocity

When an object moves around a circular path at a steady speed $v$, its angular displacement $\theta$ increases at a steady rate. We say that it has a constant angular velocity $\omega$ (Greek letter omega). **Angular velocity** is the rate at which the object's angular displacement changes. If the object moves through an angle $\theta$ in time $t$, then its angular velocity is given by:

$$\omega = \frac{\theta}{t}$$

So if an object moves through 1 radian each second, its angular velocity is $1\,\mathrm{rad\,s^{-1}}$. (Note that we are only considering an object moving at a steady rate around a circle, so that its angular velocity is constant.)

## *Angular velocity and speed*

We can now relate the angular velocity $\omega$ of the moving object to its speed $v$. If we combine the equations $\theta = s/r$ and $\omega = \theta/t$, we can eliminate $\theta$:

$$\omega = \frac{s}{rt} \quad \text{or} \quad r\omega = \frac{s}{t}$$

But $s/t$ is the speed $v$ of the moving object. So we have:

$$v = r\omega$$

So the speed of the moving object depends on its angular velocity (the rate at which it is going around the circle) and the radius of its orbit. This makes sense if you think about the motion of the second hand of a clock *(figure 1.5)*. All points along the hand have the same angular velocity, but the end of the hand is moving faster than any other point along its length.

It is important to note that, when discussing circular motion, we use $v$ to represent the speed of the moving object – a scalar quantity, the direction of which is always changing. In linear motion, we use $v$ to mean velocity, a vector quantity.

● *Figure 1.5* The end of the second hand moves fastest.

## SAQ 1.5

Calculate the angular velocities (in $\mathrm{rad\,s^{-1}}$) of the second, minute and hour hands of a clock.

## SAQ 1.6

The Earth rotates once on its axis in 24 hours. Its radius is 6400 km.

**a** Calculate the angular velocity (in $\mathrm{rad\,s^{-1}}$) of any point on the Earth's surface.

**b** Calculate the speed (in $\mathrm{m\,s^{-1}}$) of a point on the equator.

# Centripetal force and acceleration

Any object moving along a circular path has a changing velocity, even if its speed is constant. It is being accelerated towards the centre of the circle, and we say that it has a **centripetal acceleration** $a$. There must be some force which is causing this acceleration; there is a **centripetal force** $F$ pulling the object towards the centre of the circle *(figure 1.6)*.

You should recall that the word 'centripetal' is an adjective, used to describe the fact that $a$ and $F$

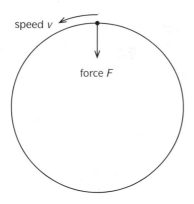

speed *v*

force *F*

● **Figure 1.6** Any object moving at a steady speed around a circle must have an unbalanced, centripetal force acting on it.

are directed towards the centre of the circle. The force can arise in many different ways. It may be caused by the tension in a string, or by gravitational attraction, or by friction. In our present analysis, we are not particularly concerned with the origin of the force.

The centripetal acceleration of an object moving with speed $v$ in an orbit of radius $r$ is given by:

$$a = \frac{v^2}{r}$$

If we eliminate $v$ using $v = r\omega$, we obtain:

$$a = r\omega^2$$

If the moving object has mass $m$, we can find the centripetal force needed to produce this acceleration by using $F = ma$:

$$F = mr\omega^2$$

(Recall that $F$ can also be calculated using $F = mv^2/r$.)

We shall now do an example. A racing car of mass 800 kg travels once around a level circular track of radius 200 m in 30 s. Calculate the car's angular velocity and centripetal acceleration, and the frictional force needed to produce this acceleration.

Since the car travels once around the track ($\theta = 2\pi$ rad) in 30 s, we can calculate $\omega$:

$$\omega = \frac{2\pi \, \text{rad}}{30 \, \text{s}}$$
$$= 0.21 \, \text{rad s}^{-1}$$

Now we can find its centripetal acceleration:

$$a = r\omega^2$$
$$= 200 \, \text{m} \times (0.21 \, \text{rad s}^{-1})^2$$
$$= 8.8 \, \text{m s}^{-2}$$

and the necessary centripetal force:

$$F = ma$$
$$= 800 \, \text{kg} \times 8.8 \, \text{m s}^{-2}$$
$$= 7040 \, \text{N}$$

Note that we could have calculated $a$ and $F$ by first finding $v$ rather than $\omega$. Note also that the acceleration has a value approaching $g$ (= 9.81 m s$^{-2}$), the acceleration of an object falling freely under gravity near the Earth's surface. This is a large acceleration for a car, more than you would normally experience during everyday motoring. Racing drivers, the crews of military jets and astronauts at lift-off may be subjected to accelerations of several $g$, something which most of us rarely undergo.

### SAQ 1.7

Following the worked example above, calculate the car's speed $v$ around the track, using $v = r\omega$. Then calculate its centripetal acceleration $a$ using $a = v^2/r$. (You should see that the two calculations are equivalent to one another.)

### SAQ 1.8

The Moon orbits the Earth once every 27.3 days at an average distance of 384 000 km. Its mass is $7.4 \times 10^{22}$ kg. Calculate:

**a** its angular velocity $\omega$;

**b** its centripetal acceleration $a$;

**c** the gravitational force $F$ of the Earth on the Moon.

## *The origins of centripetal forces*

It is useful to look at one or two situations where the physical origin of the centripetal force may not be immediately obvious. In each case, you will notice that the forces acting on the moving object are not balanced. An object moving along a circular path is not in equilibrium, and the resultant force acting on it is the centripetal force.

1 A car cornering on a level road (*figure 1.7*).
Here, the road provides two forces. The normal

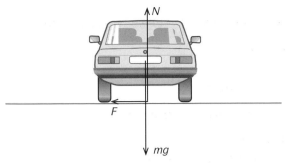

● **Figure 1.7** This car is moving away from us and turning to the left; friction provides the centripetal force. *N* and *F* are the *total* normal reaction and friction forces (respectively) provided by the contact of all four wheels with the ground.

reaction *N* is a contact force which balances the weight *mg* of the car. The second force is the force of friction *F* between the tyres and the road surface. This is the unbalanced, centripetal force. If the road or tyres do not provide enough friction, the car will not go round the bend along the desired path.

2   A car cornering on a banked road (*figure 1.8a*). Here, the normal reaction has a horizontal component which can provide the centripetal force. The vertical component of *N* balances the car's weight. We can write these two statements in the form of two equations:

$$N \sin \theta = mv^2/r$$
$$N \cos \theta = mg$$

If we divide one equation by the other, we get:

$$\frac{N \sin \theta}{N \cos \theta} = \frac{mv^2/r}{mg}$$

We can cancel both *N* and *m* to get:

$$\frac{\sin \theta}{\cos \theta} = \tan \theta = \frac{v^2}{rg}$$

so

$$v^2 = rg \tan \theta$$

This equation is used by road designers to decide on a suitable angle at which to bank a road surface. They know the radius of curvature of the road and the typical speed of traffic using the road. Then they can calculate the banking angle *θ*.

  If a car travels around the bend at a slower speed, it will tend to slide down the slope and

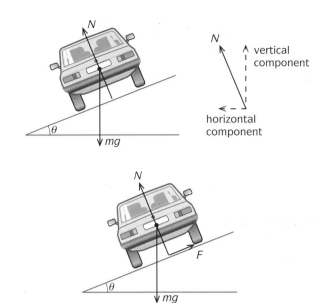

● **Figure 1.8** On a banked road, the normal reaction of the road can provide the centripetal force needed for cornering. For a slow car, friction acts up the slope to stop it from sliding down.

friction will act up the slope to keep it on course (*figure 1.8b*). If it travels too fast, it will tend to slide up the slope. If friction is insufficient, it will move up the slope and come off the road.

3   An aircraft banking (*figure 1.9a*). To change direction, the pilot tips the aircraft's wings. The vertical component of the lift force *L* on the wings balances the weight. The horizontal component of *L* provides the centripetal force.

4   A stone being whirled in a horizontal circle on the end of a string (*figure 1.9b*). The vertical and horizontal components of the tension *T* balance the weight and provide the centripetal force respectively.

5   At the fairground (*figure 1.9c*). As the cylinder spins, the floor drops away. Friction balances your weight. The normal reaction of the wall provides the centripetal force. You feel as though you are being pushed back against the wall; what you are feeling is the push of the wall on your back.

  Note that the three situations shown in *figures 1.8a, 1.9a* and *1.9b* are all equivalent. The moving object's weight acts downwards, and the second force has a vertical component, which balances the

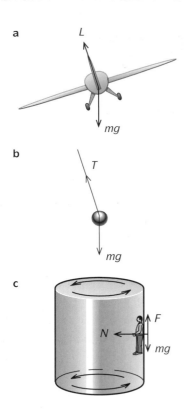

a

L

mg

b

T

mg

c

N
F
mg

● **Figure 1.9** Three more ways of providing a centripetal force.

weight, and a horizontal component, which provides the centripetal force.

## SAQ 1.9

Explain why it is impossible to whirl a conker around on the end of a string in such a way that the string remains perfectly horizontal.

## SAQ 1.10

Explain why an aircraft will tend to lose height when banking, unless the pilot increases its speed to provide more lift.

## SAQ 1.11

An aircraft is flying along a straight, horizontal path at $200\,\mathrm{m\,s^{-1}}$. The pilot tilts the wings through an angle of $10°$. What is the radius of the circular path which the plane will follow?

# SUMMARY

■ The angular displacement $\theta$ of an object moving in a circle is a measure of the angle through which the object has moved around its orbit. It is useful to measure angular displacement in radians.

■ The angular velocity $\omega$ of a body is the rate at which its angular displacement changes.

■ We can express speed, acceleration and force in terms of angular velocity:
- speed $\qquad\qquad\qquad v = r\omega$
- centripetal acceleration $\quad a = r\omega^2$
- centripetal force $\qquad\quad F = mr\omega^2$

$\omega = \dfrac{\theta}{t}$

$s = r\theta$

# $\mathcal{Q}$uestions

1  What is the angular velocity (in radians per hour) of the Sun as it moves across the sky?

2  A student whirls a $100\,\mathrm{g}$ mass around on the end of a string $0.3\,\mathrm{m}$ long. It makes 20 complete revolutions in $5.0\,\mathrm{s}$. Calculate:
   a  its angular velocity;     b  its speed;
   c  its centripetal acceleration;     d  the tension in the string.

3  A car of mass $1000\,\mathrm{kg}$ is travelling around a bend on a level road. It completes the $120°$ bend in $15\,\mathrm{s}$. The radius of curvature of the bend is $250\,\mathrm{m}$. Calculate the frictional force between the tyres and the road surface.

4  The Moon orbits the Earth with a centripetal acceleration of $0.0025\,\mathrm{m\,s^{-2}}$ at a distance of $400\,000\,\mathrm{km}$. Calculate:
   a  its angular velocity;
   b  the time it takes to orbit the Earth once.

5  If you have ever been down a water-slide (a flume) *(figure 1.10)* you will know that you tend to slide up the side as you go around a bend. Explain how this provides the centripetal force needed to push you around the bend. Why do you slide higher if you are going faster?

● **Figure 1.10** Going round the bend on a water-slide.

## Chapter two

# Orbiting under gravity

**By the end of this chapter you should be able to:**

1 analyse circular orbits in gravitational fields by relating the gravitational force to the centripetal acceleration it causes;

2 understand geostationary orbits and describe their applications.

## Gravity as a centripetal force

For an object orbiting a planet, such as a satellite orbiting the Earth, gravity provides the centripetal force which keeps it in orbit *(figure 2.1)*. In this case, we have a simple situation in that there is only one force acting – the gravitational attraction of the Earth on the satellite – and this must be the force which makes the satellite follow a circular path.

Newton's law of gravitation gives us an expression for the force between two objects whose masses are $m_1$ and $m_2$, separated by a distance $r$:

$$F = -G\frac{m_1 m_2}{r^2}$$

where $G$ is the gravitational constant. The force obeys an inverse square law. Since this provides the centripetal force acting on the satellite (mass $m_2$), we can write:

$$-G\frac{m_1 m_2}{r^2} = -\frac{m_2 v^2}{r}$$

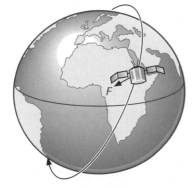

● *Figure 2.1* The gravitational attraction of the Earth provides the centripetal force on an orbiting satellite.

Cancelling and rearranging gives

$$v^2 = G\frac{m_1}{r} \qquad\qquad (2.1)$$

This equation allows us to calculate, for example, the speed at which a satellite must travel to stay in a circular orbit. Notice that the mass of the satellite, $m_2$, has cancelled out. The implication of this is that all satellites, whatever their masses, will travel at the same speed in a particular orbit. You would find this very reassuring if you were an astronaut on a space walk outside your spacecraft *(figure 2.2)*. You would travel at the same speed as your craft, despite the fact that your mass is a lot less than its mass.

Consider this example. The Moon orbits the Earth at an average distance of 384 000 km. Calculate its speed, given that the mass of Earth is $6.0 \times 10^{24}$ kg and the gravitational constant $G$ is $6.67 \times 10^{-11}$ N m$^2$ kg$^{-2}$.

Using $v^2 = Gm_1/r$ we have:

$$v^2 = \frac{6.67 \times 10^{-11}\,\text{N m}^2\text{kg}^{-2} \times 6.0 \times 10^{24}\,\text{kg}}{3.84 \times 10^8\,\text{m}}$$

$$= 1.04 \times 10^6\,\text{m}^2\text{s}^{-2}$$

So $v = 1020\,\text{m s}^{-1}$

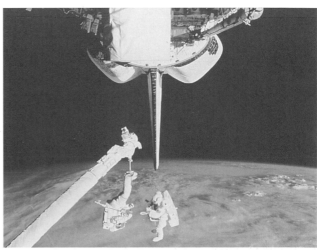

● *Figure 2.2* During this space walk, both the astronauts and the spacecraft travel through space at over 8 km per second.

**SAQ 2.1**

Calculate the orbital speed of a satellite travelling 200 km above the Earth's surface. (Radius of Earth = $6.4 \times 10^6$ m; mass of Earth = $6.0 \times 10^{24}$ kg; gravitational constant $G = 6.67 \times 10^{-11}$ N m$^2$ kg$^{-2}$.)

| Planet | $r$/m | $T$/s | $r^3$/m$^3$ | $T^2$/s$^2$ |
|---|---|---|---|---|
| Mercury | $5.8 \times 10^{10}$ | $7.6 \times 10^6$ | $2.0 \times 10^{32}$ | $5.8 \times 10^{13}$ |
| Venus | $1.1 \times 10^{11}$ | $1.9 \times 10^7$ | $1.3 \times 10^{33}$ | $3.6 \times 10^{14}$ |
| Earth | $1.5 \times 10^{11}$ | $3.2 \times 10^7$ | $3.4 \times 10^{33}$ | $1.0 \times 10^{15}$ |
| Mars | $2.3 \times 10^{11}$ | $5.9 \times 10^7$ | $1.2 \times 10^{34}$ | $3.5 \times 10^{15}$ |

● **Table 2.1** Data for the four planets closest to the Sun

# The orbital period

It is often more useful to consider the time taken for a complete orbit, the orbital period $T$. Since the distance around an orbit is $2\pi r$, it follows that:

$$v = \frac{2\pi r}{T}$$

Substituting in *equation 2.1* gives:

$$\frac{4\pi^2 r^2}{T^2} = G\frac{m_1}{r}$$

$$\text{or} \quad T^2 = \frac{4\pi^2 r^3}{Gm_1} \quad (2.2)$$

This equation tells us how the orbital period is related to the radius of the orbit. The square of

the period is proportional to the cube of the radius ($T^2 \propto r^3$). This is an important result. It was first discovered by Johannes Kepler (*figure 2.3*), who analysed the available data for the planets of the solar system. It was an empirical law (a law based solely on experiment) since he had no theory to explain why there should be this relationship between $T$ and $r$. It was not until Isaac Newton devised his law of gravitation that it was possible to explain the relationship, which is known as one of Kepler's laws of planetary motion. Explaining Kepler's law was one of the triumphs of Newton's theory. (See the *Cosmology* book in this series for more about these laws.)

*Table 2.1* shows values of $T$ and $r$ for the four planets of the solar system that are closest to the Sun. The values of $T^2$ and $r^3$ are plotted in *figure 2.4*. The gradient of this graph can be used to determine the mass of the Sun, as follows:

$$\text{gradient} = \frac{T^2}{r^3} = \frac{4\pi^2}{Gm_1} = 3.0 \times 10^{-19}\,\text{s}^2\text{m}^{-3}$$

Hence

$$m_1 = \frac{4\pi^2}{G \times \text{gradient}} = 2.0 \times 10^{30}\,\text{kg}$$

● **Figure 2.3** Johannes Kepler, who devised mathematical laws to describe the motion of the planets.

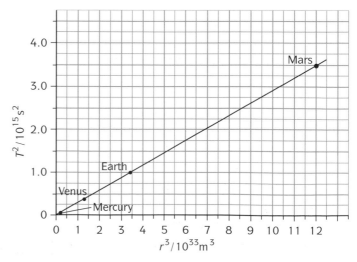

● **Figure 2.4** A graph to show the validity of Kepler's law for the first four planets.

## Jupiter's moons

● *Figure 2.5* Jupiter and four of its moons, as seen by Voyager 1; this is a composite photograph.

Jupiter has many moons which orbit it *(figure 2.5)*. Four were observed by Galileo Galilei in 1610, and others have been discovered since. *Table 2.2* shows the orbital periods and distances from Jupiter of Galileo's moons.

**A** Use these data to check that they follow Kepler's law ($T^2 \propto r^3$). Deduce the mass of Jupiter.

**B** The American astronomer Edward Emerson Barnard observed a fifth moon, Amalthea, in 1892. Its orbital period is 0.50 days. Calculate the radius of its orbit around Jupiter.

| Moon | $r$/m | $T$/days |
|------|-------|----------|
| Io | $4.2 \times 10^8$ | 1.77 |
| Europa | $6.7 \times 10^8$ | 3.55 |
| Ganymede | $1.1 \times 10^9$ | 7.2 |
| Callisto | $1.9 \times 10^9$ | 16.7 |

● *Table 2.2* The moons of Jupiter observed by Galileo

# Earth orbit

The Earth has one natural satellite – the Moon – and many thousands of artificial satellites. Each of these satellites uses the Earth's gravitational field to provide the centripetal force that keeps it in orbit. In order for a satellite to maintain a particular orbit, it must travel at the correct speed. This is given by *equation 2.1* (derived earlier):

$$v^2 = G \frac{m_1}{r}$$

It follows from this equation that the closer the satellite is to the Earth, the faster it must travel. If it travels too slowly, it will fall down towards the Earth's surface. If it travels too quickly, it will move outwards into a higher orbit.

## SAQ 2.2

A satellite orbiting a few hundred kilometres above the Earth's surface will experience a slight frictional drag from the Earth's (very thin) atmosphere. Draw a diagram to show how you would expect the satellite's orbit to change as a result. How can this problem be overcome?

## *Observing the Earth*

Artificial satellites have a variety of uses. Many are used for making observations of the Earth's surface for commercial, environmental, meteorological and military purposes. Others are used for astronomical observations; they benefit greatly from being above the Earth's atmosphere. Still others are used for navigation and telecommunications.

A satellite close to the Earth's surface travels fast, and completes each orbit in about 90 minutes. Such a satellite might follow an orbit that takes it over the poles *(figure 2.6)*. Because the satellite is close to the Earth's surface, it cannot 'see' a large area at any one time. However, the Earth is turning under the satellite, which therefore 'sees' a different strip of the surface during each orbit. In 24 hours it completes about 16 orbits, and a

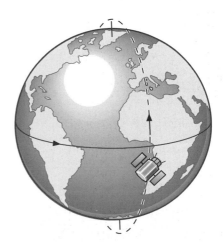

● *Figure 2.6* An over-the-poles orbit for a satellite in near-Earth orbit. The Earth turns beneath the satellite as it orbits.

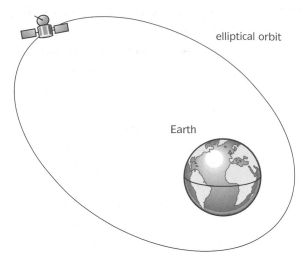

elliptical orbit

Earth

● *Figure 2.7* Some satellites follow highly elliptical orbits around the Earth.

● *Figure 2.8* An image of part of the Earth's surface, obtained from a remote-sensing satellite.

picture of the whole of the Earth's surface can be built up.

Other satellites follow elliptical orbits that take them high up above the Earth (*figure 2.7*). The higher they are, the slower they move, and so they spend a lot of their time above one area of the Earth's surface. Although they have a more distant view of the Earth, this can be compensated for by the longer time for which they can view a particular area. Such satellites are useful for mobile phone systems in countries close to the poles.

Satellites have provided detailed views of the Earth's surface, such as that shown in *figure 2.8*. By analysing reflected light at different wavelengths, it is possible to build up a detailed picture of the vegetation and land use over much of the Earth.

A network of navigation satellites has been established, high above the Earth's surface. At any point on the Earth, an observer can have a direct view of several of these. An electronic 'sextant' receives signals from which it can deduce its distance from each satellite, and hence its position on the ground. This system is now so accurate that the observer's position can be found to within a few centimetres. This system was set up for military use, and has also proved valuable for navigation at sea and for archaeological surveying, and is even used by orienteering enthusiasts.

## Geostationary orbits

A special type of orbit is one in which a satellite is positioned so that, as it orbits, the Earth rotates below it at the same rate. The satellite remains above a fixed point on the Earth's surface. This kind of orbit is called a **geostationary orbit,** and the idea was first suggested in 1945 by the engineer and science-fiction writer Arthur C Clarke. He proposed setting up a series of communications satellites in a 'Clarke belt' above the equator. These would be used to allow telecommunications signals to leap-frog around the world.

We can work out the position of the Clarke belt using *equation 2.2*:

$$T^2 = \frac{4\pi^2 r^3}{Gm_1}$$

For a satellite to stay above a fixed point on the equator, it must take exactly 24 hours to complete one orbit (*figure 2.9*). We can find the radius $r$ of this orbit by substituting appropriate values in *equation 2.2*:

$$G = 6.67 \times 10^{-11}\,\text{N}\,\text{m}^2\text{kg}^{-2}$$
$$T = 24 \text{ hours} = 86\,400\,\text{s}$$
$$m_1 = 6.0 \times 10^{24}\text{kg}$$

Hence

$$r^3 = G\,\frac{m_1 T^2}{4\pi^2} = 7.66 \times 10^{22}\,\text{m}^3$$

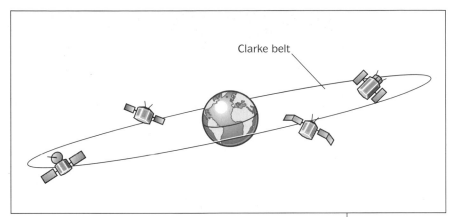

● **Figure 2.9** Geostationary satellites are parked in the Clarke belt, high above the equator.

and

$$r = 4.23 \times 10^7 \text{m}$$

So for a satellite to occupy a geostationary orbit, it must be at a distance of 42 300 km from the centre of the Earth, and at a point directly above the equator. Notice that the radius of the Earth is 6400 km, so the orbital radius is between 6 and 7 Earth radii, and *figure 2.9* has been drawn to give an impression of the size of the orbit.

## SAQ 2.3

For any future mission to Mars, it would be desirable to set up a system of three or four geostationary satellites to allow communication between the planet and Earth. Calculate the radius of a geostationary orbit around Mars. (Mass of Mars = $6.4 \times 10^{23}$ kg; period of rotation $T = 24.6$ hours; $G = 6.67 \times 10^{-11}$ N m$^2$ kg$^{-2}$.)

A geostationary orbit is sometimes known as a parking orbit. There are now over 300 satellites in such orbits. They are used for telecommunications (transmitting telephone messages around the world) and for satellite television transmission. A base station on Earth sends the television signal up to the satellite, where it is amplified and broadcast back to the ground. Satellite receiver dishes are now a familiar sight; you will have observed how they all point towards the same point in the sky. Because the satellite is in a geostationary orbit, the dish can be fixed. Satellites in any other orbits move across the sky, and a tracking system is necessary to communicate with them. Such a system is complex and expensive, and too demanding for the domestic market.

Geostationary satellites have a lifetime of perhaps ten years. They need a fuel supply to maintain them in the correct orbit, and to keep them pointing correctly towards the Earth. Eventually they run out of fuel, and they need to be replaced.

In January 1995, Arthur C Clarke was awarded an honorary degree by the University of Liverpool for his life's work in space technology. He did not attend the ceremony in person; instead, he appeared on a screen, in images beamed to Liverpool from his home in Sri Lanka via one of the geostationary satellites that he had proposed 50 years earlier.

## SUMMARY

■ A satellite in orbit around a mass is acted on by a gravitational force, which gives it a centripetal acceleration.

■ The period of the satellite's orbit can be found by equating the gravitational force $Gm_1m_2/r^2$ to the centripetal force $mv^2/r$.

■ A satellite in a geostationary orbit has a period equal to the period of rotation of the Earth. It has a fixed position in the sky.

■ Geostationary satellites are used for telecommunications transmissions and for satellite television broadcasting.

## Questions

1 The gravitational force on a satellite causes it to have a centripetal acceleration. Using this idea, show that, for a satellite orbiting a planet of mass $M$, its orbital speed $v$ is related to the diameter $d$ of its orbit by:

$$v^2 = 2G\frac{M}{d}$$

2 Explain why satellites might be useful to the following people:
   a meteorologists;
   b oil prospectors;
   c television journalists covering a war.

3 The first suggestion that Mars might have satellites (moons) was made by Jonathan Swift in *Gulliver's Travels*, published in 1727. The first satellite of Mars was not observed until 150 years later, in 1877. Now we know that there are two satellites of Mars, Phobos and Deimos. Details of their orbits are given in the *table*. Use these data to show that their orbits are consistent with Kepler's law ($T^2 \propto r^3$). Deduce the mass of Mars. (Gravitational constant $G = 6.67 \times 10^{-11}\,\mathrm{N\,m^2\,kg^{-2}}$.)

| Moon | Radius of orbit r/km | Orbital period T/days |
|---|---|---|
| Phobos | 9 270 | 0.319 |
| Deimos | 23 400 | 1.262 |

4 In a neutral hydrogen atom, a single electron orbits a single proton at a distance of $3.7 \times 10^{-11}\,\mathrm{m}$. The electrostatic force of attraction between them obeys an inverse square law (like the law of gravitation), and its value is $1.7 \times 10^{-7}\,\mathrm{N}$. This provides the centripetal force which keeps the electron in its orbit. The electron's mass is $9.11 \times 10^{-31}\,\mathrm{kg}$.

   a Calculate the electron's orbital speed and its orbital period.
   b If the orbital radius increased, predict whether these quantities would increase or decrease.

# Simple harmonic motion

## Oscillations all around

There are many situations where we can observe the special kind of oscillations called simple harmonic motion (s.h.m.). Some are more obvious than others. For example, the vibrating strings of a musical instrument *(figure 3.1)* show s.h.m. When plucked or bowed, the strings move back and forth about the midpoint of their oscillation. Such mechanical oscillations can also be seen elsewhere: in the vibrations of machinery, in the swaying of trees in the wind, in the motion of waves on the sea, and so on.

Here are some other, less obvious, situations where simple harmonic motion can be found.

■ When a sound wave travels through air, the molecules of the air vibrate back and forth with s.h.m.

■ When an alternating current flows in a wire, the electrons in the wire move with s.h.m. – see chapter 9.

■ There is a small alternating electric current in a radio or television aerial when it is tuned to a signal, in the form of electrons moving with s.h.m.

■ Any electromagnetic waves such as light or radio waves (see chapter 5) consist of simple harmonic vibrations of both electric and magnetic fields.

■ The atoms which make up a molecule vibrate with s.h.m. (see for example the hydrogen molecule in *figure 3.2a*).

■ If atoms, ions or molecules are combined to form a large-scale structure such as a crystal *(figure 3.2b)*, this structure vibrates with s.h.m.

Many of these oscillations can be very complex, because there may be many different frequencies of oscillation occurring at the same time. It is possible to break down a complex oscillation into a sum of simple oscillations, and so we will focus our attention in this chapter on s.h.m. with only one frequency. We will also concentrate on large-scale

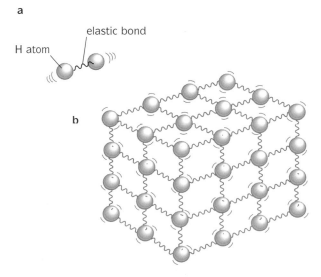

**a**

elastic bond

H atom

**b**

● *Figure 3.2* We can think of the bonds between atoms as being springy; this leads to vibrations in **a** a molecule of hydrogen and **b** a solid crystal.

● *Figure 3.1* Six simple harmonic oscillators – the strings of a guitar vibrate with s.h.m.

mechanical oscillations, but you should bear in mind that this analysis can be extended to the situations mentioned above, and many more besides.

# The requirements for s.h.m.

If a simple pendulum is undisturbed, it is in equilibrium. To start it swinging *(figure 3.3)*, it must be pulled to one side. Gravity pulls on the mass, and this force moves the mass back to its central equilibrium position. The mass swings past the midpoint until it comes to rest momentarily at the other side; the process is then repeated in the opposite direction. Note that a complete oscillation is from right to left and back again. The three requirements for s.h.m. are:

1 a mass which oscillates;
2 a central position where the mass is in equilibrium

(conventionally, displacements to the right of this position are taken as positive, to the left they are negative);

3 a restoring force which acts to return the mass to the central position (the restoring force is greater the further the mass is from equilibrium).

## SAQ 3.1
Identify the features of the motion of the simple pendulum that satisfy the three requirements for s.h.m.

# The changes of velocity in s.h.m.

As the pendulum swings back and forth, its velocity is constantly changing. As it swings from right to left (as shown in *figure 3.3*) its velocity is negative. It speeds up towards the central position, and then slows down as it approaches the other end of the oscillation. It has positive velocity as it swings back from left to right. Again, it is travelling fastest at the midpoint, and slows down as it swings up to its starting position.

This pattern of speeding up – slowing down – reversing – speeding up again is characteristic of simple harmonic motion. There are no sudden changes of velocity. Note also that, because its velocity is always changing, the mass must be accelerating and decelerating all the time. In the next section we will see how we can observe these changes, and how we can represent them graphically.

# Graphical representations

If you set up a trolley tethered between springs *(figure 3.4)* you can hear the characteristic rhythm of s.h.m. as the trolley oscillates back and forth. By adjusting the load, you can achieve oscillations with a period of about two seconds.

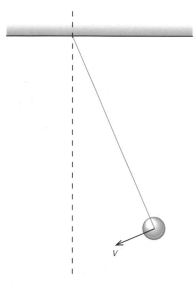

● *Figure 3.3* This pendulum has positive displacement and negative velocity.

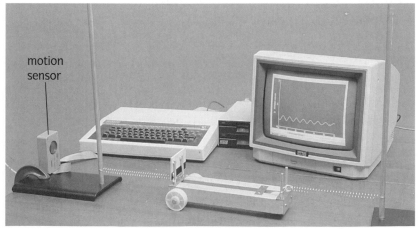

● *Figure 3.4* Using a motion sensor to measure s.h.m. of a spring–trolley system.

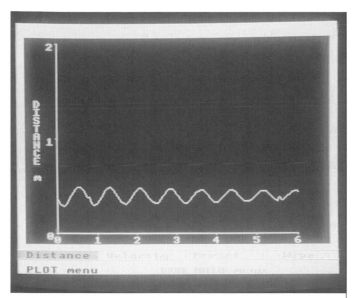

● *Figure 3.5* The screen display for a motion sensor detecting s.h.m.

The motion sensor allows you to record how the displacement of the trolley varies with time. Ultrasonic pulses from the sensor are reflected by the card on the trolley, and the reflected pulses are detected. This 'sonar' technique allows the sensor to determine the displacement of the trolley. A typical screen display is shown in *figure 3.5*.

The computer can then determine the velocity of the trolley by calculating the rate of change of displacement. Similarly, it can calculate the rate of change of velocity to determine the acceleration.

Idealised graphs of displacement, velocity and acceleration against time are shown in *figure 3.6*; we will examine these graphs in sequence to see what they tell us about s.h.m. and how the three graphs are related to one another.

■ *Displacement–time (x–t) graph*
The displacement of the oscillating mass varies according to the smooth curve shown in *figure 3.6a*. (Mathematically, this is a sine curve; its variation is described as sinusoidal.) Note that this graph allows us to determine the amplitude and the period of the oscillations.

In this graph, the displacement $x$ of the oscillation is shown as zero at the start (when $t$ is zero). We have chosen to consider the motion to start when the mass is at the midpoint of its oscillation and is moving to the right. We could

have chosen any other point in the cycle as the starting point, but it is conventional to start as shown here.

■ *Velocity–time (v–t) graph*
Again, we have a smooth curve (*figure 3.6b*), which shows how the velocity $v$ depends on time $t$. The shape of the curve is the same as for the displacement–time graph, but it starts at a different point in the cycle. When $t$ is zero, the mass is at the midpoint of its oscillation, and this is where it is moving fastest. Hence the velocity has its maximum value at this point. Its value is positive, since it is moving towards the right.

■ *Acceleration–time (a–t) graph*
Finally, we have a third curve of the same general form (*figure 3.6c*) which shows how the acceleration $a$ depends on time $t$. At the start of the oscillation, the mass is at the midpoint, where it is in equilibrium. Since there is no resultant force acting on it, its acceleration is

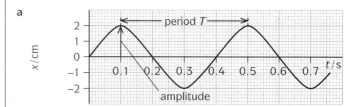

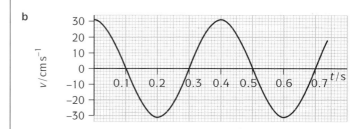

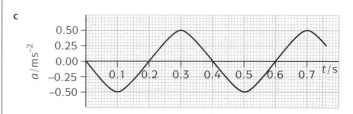

● *Figure 3.6* Displacement, velocity and acceleration graphs for s.h.m.

zero. As it moves to the right, the restoring force acts towards the left, giving it a negative acceleration. The acceleration has its greatest value when the mass is displaced furthest from the equilibrium position. Notice that, whenever the mass has a positive displacement (to the right), its acceleration is to the left, and vice versa. Hence the acceleration graph is an upside-down version of the displacement graph.

### SAQ 3.2

Use the graphs shown in *figure 3.6* to determine the values of the following quantities: **a** amplitude, **b** period, **c** maximum velocity and **d** maximum acceleration.

### SAQ 3.3

At what point in an oscillation does a mass have zero velocity but positive acceleration?

## Relating the graphs

Displacement, velocity and acceleration are related as follows:

velocity = rate of change of displacement
acceleration = rate of change of velocity

So we can deduce the velocity from the gradient of the *x*–*t* graph, and the acceleration from the gradient of the *v*–*t* graph. We can see these relationships at work if we compare the three graphs shown in *figure 3.6*.

Consider the *x*–*t* graph and the *v*–*t* graph. You should be able to see that, wherever the gradient of the *x*–*t* graph is positive, the velocity is positive. Wherever the gradient of the *x*–*t* graph is negative, the velocity is negative.

The *v*–*t* and *a*–*t* graphs are related similarly. Wherever the gradient of the *v*–*t* graph is positive, the acceleration is positive. Wherever the gradient of the *v*–*t* graph is negative, the acceleration is negative.

### SAQ 3.4

Look at the *x*–*t* graph *(figure 3.6a)*. When $t = 0.1$ s, what is the gradient of the graph? What does this tell you about the velocity at this instant?

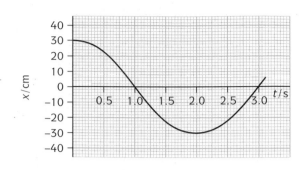

● **Figure 3.7** A displacement–time graph.

### SAQ 3.5

*Fgure 3.7* shows how the displacement of an oscillating mass changes with time. Use the graph to deduce the following quantities:

**a** the velocity when $t = 0$ s;

**b** the maximum velocity;

**c** the acceleration when $t = 1$ s.

# Frequency and angular frequency

The frequency $f$ of s.h.m. tells us how many cycles of the oscillations take place in each second. It is related to the period $T$ by:

$$f = \frac{1}{T}$$

We can think of a complete cycle of s.h.m. as being represented by $2\pi$ radians. (Recall that, in a complete cycle of circular motion, an object moves round through $2\pi$ rad.) We say that the phase of the oscillation varies by $2\pi$ rad during one cycle. Hence, if there are $f$ cycles in 1 s, we can say that there are $2\pi f$ rad in 1 s. This quantity is the angular frequency of the s.h.m. and it is represented by the symbol $\omega$, in just the same way that angular velocity is in the case of circular motion.

Angular frequency is thus related to frequency and period as follows:

$$\omega = 2\pi f = \frac{2\pi}{T} \quad \text{or} \quad T = \frac{2\pi}{\omega}$$

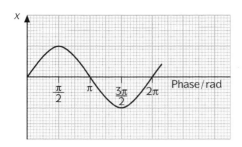

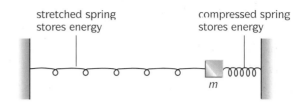

● *Figure 3.8* The phase of an oscillation varies from 0 to $2\pi$ during one cycle.

In *figure 3.8*, a single cycle of s.h.m. is shown, but with the *x* axis marked with the phase of the motion in radians.

## Circular motion and s.h.m.

There is a close relationship between circular motion and s.h.m. One way to see this is to picture a turntable, turning at a steady speed with angular velocity $\omega$ *(figure 3.9a)*. When viewed from above, the marker X moves round at a steady speed. However, if viewed from the side as in *figure 3.9b*, the marker moves with apparent s.h.m. It shows the speeding up – slowing down behaviour characteristic of s.h.m., and its angular frequency is $\omega$.

### SAQ 3.6

An object moving with s.h.m. goes through two complete cycles in 1 s. Calculate the values of: **a** *T*, **b** *f*, **c** $\omega$.

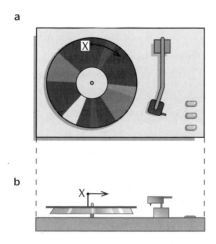

● *Figure 3.9* A turntable viewed from above, **a**, shows circular motion, but from the side, **b**, it shows apparent s.h.m.

● *Figure 3.10* The elastic potential energy stored in the springs is converted to kinetic energy when the mass is released.

# Energy

During simple harmonic motion, there is a constant interchange of energy between two forms: potential and kinetic. We can see this by considering the mass–spring system shown in *figure 3.10*. When the mass is pulled to one side (to start the oscillations), one spring is compressed and the other is stretched. The springs store elastic potential energy. When the mass is released, it moves back towards the central position, accelerating as it goes. It has increasing kinetic energy. The potential energy stored in the springs decreases, and the kinetic energy of the mass increases by a corresponding amount. Once the mass has passed the midpoint of its oscillation, its kinetic energy decreases and the energy is transferred back to the springs. Provided the oscillations are undamped, the total energy in the system remains constant.

## Energy graphs

We can represent these energy changes in two ways. *Figure 3.11* shows how the two forms of

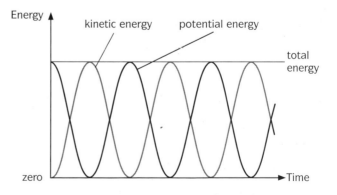

● *Figure 3.11* The kinetic and potential energy of an oscillator vary periodically, but the total energy remains constant if the system is undamped.

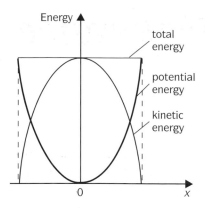

● *Figure 3.12* The kinetic energy is maximum at zero displacement; potential energy is maximum at maximum displacement.

energy change with time during two complete cycles. Potential energy is maximum when displacement is maximum (positive or negative); kinetic energy is maximum when displacement is zero. Total energy remains constant throughout. A second way to show this is to draw a graph of how potential and kinetic energy vary with displacement (*figure 3.12*). You should see that this shows the same variation as in *figure 3.11*.

## SAQ 3.7

To start a pendulum swinging, you pull it slightly to one side.

**a** What kind of energy does this transfer to the mass?

**b** Describe the energy changes that occur when the mass is released.

## SAQ 3.8

*Figure 3.12* shows how the different forms of energy change with displacement during s.h.m. Copy the graph, and show how the graph would differ if the oscillating mass were given only half the initial input of energy.

## SUMMARY

■ Simple harmonic motion is a form of oscillatory motion characterised by a sinusoidal variation of displacement, velocity and acceleration with time.

■ For a body to execute s.h.m., it must be subject to a restoring force which is proportional to its displacement from a fixed, equilibrium position.

■ During a single cycle of s.h.m., the phase varies through $2\pi$ radians. The angular frequency $\omega$ of the motion is related to its period $T$ by $T = 2\pi/\omega$.

■ In s.h.m., there is a regular interchange between kinetic energy and potential energy.

## Questions

1 Explain why the motion of someone jumping up and down on a trampoline is not simple harmonic motion. (Their feet lose contact with the trampoline during each bounce.)

2 An atom in a crystal vibrates back and forth with a frequency of $10^{14}$ Hz. The amplitude of its motion is $2 \times 10^{-12}$ m.
 **a** Sketch a graph to show how the displacement of the atom varies during one cycle of its simple harmonic motion.
 **b** Use your graph to estimate the atom's greatest speed.

3 The pendulum of a grandfather clock swings from one side to the other in 1 s. Calculate: **a** the period of the motion, **b** the frequency and **c** the angular frequency.

4 *Figure 3.13* shows how the velocity of a 2 kg mass was found to vary during an investigation of the simple harmonic motion of a pendulum. Use the graph to estimate:
 **a** the mass's greatest velocity;
 **b** its greatest kinetic energy;
 **c** its greatest potential energy;
 **d** its greatest acceleration;
 **e** the greatest restoring force that acted on it.

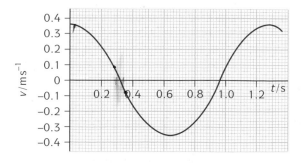

● *Figure 3.13* A velocity–time graph.

## Chapter four

# The diffraction and interference of light

## By the end of this chapter you should be able to:

1 recall and use the equation $\lambda = ax/D$ for double-slit interference of light;

2 describe an experiment to determine the wavelength of light using a double-slit interference method;

3 recall the formula $d \sin \theta = n\lambda$ and describe the use of a diffraction grating to determine the wavelength of light.

For a long time in the seventeenth and eighteenth centuries, scientists debated the nature of light. Did light travel in the form of corpuscles (particles) or as waves? Newton favoured the corpuscular theory, because of the way in which light travels in straight lines. However, evidence accumulated which suggested that light was indeed some form of wave disturbance. In particular, when light was shone on an object, interference fringes were observed at the edge of its shadow. This was difficult to achieve three hundred years ago; nowadays we can use lasers to see some spectacular interference effects such as that shown in *figure 4.1*.

You should recall the meanings of the following terms.

■ *Diffraction*
The spreading out of waves as they pass through a gap in a barrier, or past the edge of an object. The effect is significant when the wavelength of the waves is similar to the width of the gap.

■ *Interference*
When two or more sets of waves arrive together at a point, they may interfere in such a way as to cancel out (destructive interference) or give a larger amplitude wave (constructive interference).

■ *Superposition*
When two or more waves coincide, we can find the displacement of the resultant wave simply by adding up the separate displacements of the individual waves. This is the *principle of superposition*.

These phenomena apply to waves but not to particles. Hence if we can observe diffraction and interference, we can conclude that we are observing a wave phenomenon.

## Double-slit interference

By the end of the eighteenth century, physicists had developed considerable skill in optics. Thomas Young set out to perform an experiment which would provide incontrovertible proof of the wave nature of light. This was his double-slit interference experiment, which can be performed using a laser (*figure 4.2*), though of course Young did not have access to a laser in his time.

The double slit is provided by a slide that is black apart from two parallel, transparent slits

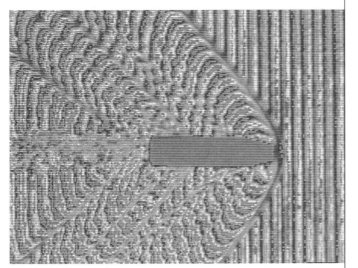

● *Figure 4.1* Because a laser is a good source of coherent light, it allows us to see interference fringes very clearly. This image shows the disturbance caused by a bullet moving at 500 m s⁻¹.

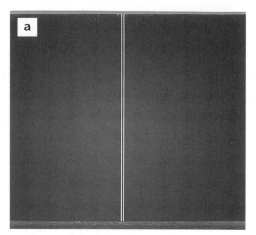

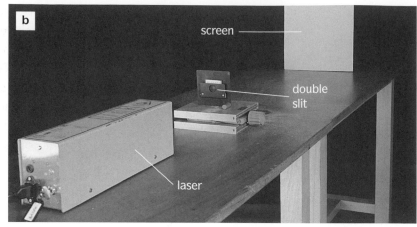

● *Figure 4.2* A laser beam shows clear interference fringes using a double-slit arrangement. **a** shows a close up of the slits; **b** shows the apparatus in use.

through which the light can pass into the space beyond. The slits are a fraction of a millimetre wide and are separated by about a millimetre.

A screen is positioned at a distance of a metre or so beyond the slits, and a pattern of interference 'fringes' appears on the screen. Fringes are regions of lightness and darkness. In this experiment, they appear as evenly spaced patches of light across the screen (*figure 4.3*). The fact that we see such an obvious interference effect means that we can conclude that, in this situation, light behaves as a wave. (This experiment is equivalent to the two-source interference experiments for ripples and for microwaves described in *Basic Physics 1 and 2*, pages 31–32 and 33.)

## *Explaining the experiment*

In order to observe interference, we need two sets of waves. They must have the same wavelength, and they must be coherent (the phase difference between them must remain constant). This is

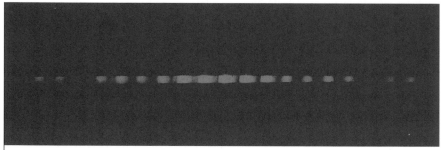

● *Figure 4.3* Interference fringes obtained using a laser and a double slit.

achieved in this experiment by passing a single beam of laser light through the two slits. As the light passes through the slits, it is diffracted so that it spreads out into the space beyond (*figure 4.4*). Now we have two overlapping sets of waves, and the pattern of fringes on the screen shows us the result of their interference.

How does this pattern arise? We will consider three points on the screen (*figure 4.5*), and work out what we would expect to observe at each.

■ *Point A*
This point is directly opposite the midpoint of the slits. Two rays of light arrive at A, one from slit 1 and the other from slit 2.

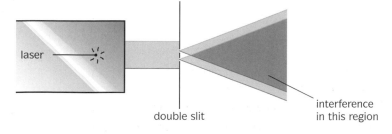

● *Figure 4.4* Interference occurs where diffracted beams from the two slits overlap.

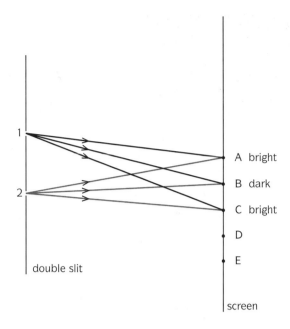

● **Figure 4.5** Rays from the two slits travel different distances to reach the screen.

Point A is equidistant from the two slits, and so the two rays of light have travelled the same distance. If we assume that they were in step (in phase) with each other when they left the slits, then they will be in step when they arrive at A. Hence they will interfere constructively, and we will observe a bright fringe at A.

■ *Point B*
This point is slightly to the side of point A, and is the midpoint of the first dark fringe. Again, two rays of light arrive at B, one from each slit. The light from slit 1 has to travel slightly further than the light from slit 2, and so the two rays are no longer in step. Since point B is at the midpoint of the dark fringe, the two rays must be exactly out of phase. Ray 1 must be half a wavelength ($\lambda/2$) behind ray 2, and so the two rays interfere destructively.

■ *Point C*
This point is the midpoint of the next bright fringe, so that AB = BC. Again, ray 1 has travelled further than ray 2; this time, it has travelled an extra distance equal to a whole wavelength ($\lambda$), and the two rays are in step at the screen. They interfere constructively and we see a bright fringe.

The complete interference pattern can be explained in this way. Where there is a bright fringe on the screen, the two rays are arriving in step. Their path lengths from the two slits differ by a whole number of wavelengths. Where there is a dark fringe, their path lengths differ by a whole number of wavelengths plus half a wavelength. (At positions in between, the path difference between the two rays involves a fraction of a wavelength, and there is partial cancelling out of the light.)

### SAQ 4.1

Consider points D and E on the screen, where BC = CD = DE. Say what you would expect to observe at D and E, and explain why.

## *Determining* $\lambda$

The double-slit experiment can be used to determine the wavelength of light, $\lambda$. The following three quantities have to be measured.

■ *Slit separation a*
This is the distance between the centres of the slits, though it may be easier to measure between the edges of the slits. (It is difficult to judge the position of the centre of a slit. If the slits are the same width, the separation of their left-hand edges is the same as the separation of their centres.) A travelling microscope is suitable for measuring $a$.

■ *Fringe separation x*
This is the distance between the centres of adjacent bright (or dark) fringes. It is best to measure across several fringes (say, ten) and then to calculate the average separation. A metre rule or travelling microscope can be used.

■ *Slit-to-screen distance D*
This is the distance from the midpoint of the slits to the central fringe on the screen. It can be measured using a metre rule.

Once these three quantities have been measured, the wavelength $\lambda$ of the light can be found using:

$$\lambda = \frac{ax}{D} \qquad (4.1)$$

We shall now do an example. In a double-slit experiment using light from a helium–neon laser, a student obtained the following results:

| width of 10 fringes | $10x = 1.5\,cm$ |
| separation of slits | $a = 1.0\,mm$ |
| slit-to-screen distance | $D = 2.40\,m$ |

Answer: fringe separation $x = 1.5\,mm$ and $\lambda = ax/D = 630\,nm$.

## SAQ 4.2

If the student in the worked example above moved the screen to a distance of 4.8 m from the slits, what would the fringe separation become? (There is no need to perform a full calculation.)

## Experimental details

An alternative arrangement for carrying out the double-slit experiment is shown in *figure 4.6*. Here, a white light source is used, rather than a laser. A single slit acts as a narrow source of light. The double slit is placed a centimetre or two beyond, and the fringes are observed on a screen a metre or so away. The experiment has to be carried out in a darkened room, as the intensity of the light is low and the fringes are hard to see. There are three important factors involved in the way the equipment is set up.

- The slits are a fraction of a millimetre in width. Since the wavelength of light is less than a micrometre, this gives a small amount of diffraction in the space beyond. If the slits were narrower, the intensity of the light would be too low for visible fringes to be achieved.

- The slits are about a millimetre apart. If they were much further apart, the fringes would be too close together to be distinguishable.
- The screen is about a metre from the slits. This gives fringes which are clearly separated without being too dim.

With a laser, the light beam is more concentrated, and the first single slit is not necessary. The greater intensity of the beam means that the screen can be further from the slits, so that the fringes are further apart; this reduces the fractional error in measurements of $x$ and $D$, and hence $\lambda$ is more accurately determined.

A laser has a second advantage. The light from a laser is monochromatic; that is, it consists of a single wavelength. This makes the fringes very clear, and many of them are formed across the screen. With white light, a range of wavelengths are present. Different wavelengths form fringes at different points across the screen. The central fringe is white (because all wavelengths are in step here), but the other fringes show coloured effects, and only a few fringes are visible in the interference pattern.

## SAQ 4.3

Use $\lambda = ax/D$ *(equation 4.1)* to explain the following observations.

a  With the slits closer together, the fringes are further apart.

b  Interference fringes for blue light are closer together than for red light.

c  In an experiment to measure the wavelength of light, it is desirable to have the screen as far from the slits as possible.

## SAQ 4.4

In a Young's slits experiment, filters were placed in front of a white light source to investigate the effect of changing the wavelength of the light. At first, a red filter was used ($\lambda = 600\,nm$), and the fringe separation was found to be 2.4 mm. A blue filter was then used ($\lambda = 450\,nm$). What would the fringe separation become?

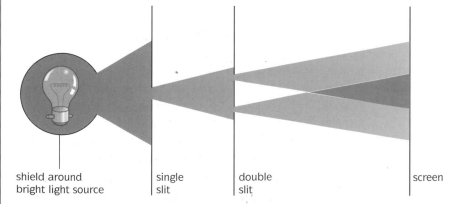

shield around | single | double | screen
bright light source | slit | slit |

● **Figure 4.6** To observe interference fringes with white light, it is necessary to use a single slit before the double slit.

## The derivation of $\lambda = ax/D$

It is useful to look at the derivation of the expression $\lambda = ax/D$, to see what conditions must apply before we can legitimately use it. *Figure 4.7* shows the same arrangement as in *figure 4.5*, with points A and C being the midpoints of the central bright fringe and the next bright fringe respectively. Points X and Y are directly opposite slits 1 and 2.

It is clear from *figure 4.7* that ray 1 has travelled further than ray 2 by the time it reaches point C. In fact, it has travelled an extra distance $\lambda$, since the two rays are interfering constructively. From the geometry of the figure, we can deduce an expression for this path difference in terms of $a$, $x$ and $D$. Each ray is the hypotenuse of a right-angled triangle; ray 1 of triangle $S_1CX$, and ray 2 of triangle $S_2CY$. Using Pythagoras' theorem, we can then write expressions for $S_1C$ and $S_2C$:

$$S_1C^2 = S_1X^2 + CX^2 = D^2 + (x + a/2)^2$$
$$S_2C^2 = S_2Y^2 + CY^2 = D^2 + (x - a/2)^2$$

Subtracting one equation from the other gives:

$$S_1C^2 - S_2C^2 = (x + a/2)^2 - (x - a/2)^2$$

Each side of this equation is the difference of two squares, and so we can write:

$$(S_1C + S_2C)(S_1C - S_2C)$$
$$= (x + a/2 + x - a/2)(x + a/2 - x + a/2)$$
$$= 2ax$$

Now, both $S_1C$ and $S_2C$ are very similar in length to the slit-to-screen distance $D$, and we can write (with only a small degree of approximation):

$$S_1C + S_2C = 2D$$

The difference between $S_1C$ and $S_2C$ is the path difference between the two rays, and this is equal to one wavelength, $\lambda$:

$$S_1C - S_2C = \lambda$$

Substituting gives:

$$2D\lambda = 2ax$$

and hence:

$$\lambda = \frac{ax}{D}$$

Note the approximation we have made: the length of each ray is almost equal to $D$. In other words, the angle each ray makes with the horizontal (in *figure 4.7*) must be very small.

### SAQ 4.5

Consider *figure 4.7*. Typical measurements are: $D = 2.0\,\text{m}$; $a = x = 1\,\text{mm}$.

a  Using these values, apply Pythagoras' theorem to calculate values for $S_1C$ and $S_2C$. Show that both are almost exactly equal to $D$.

b  Calculate the difference between $S_1C$ and $S_2C$, and show that this is comparable to the wavelength of light.

(You will need to use a calculator capable of calculating to 8 or 9 significant figures.)

# Diffraction gratings

A diffraction grating is similar to the slide used in the double-slit experiment, but with many more slits than just two. It consists of a large number of equally spaced slits ('lines') ruled on a glass or plastic slide. There may be as many as 10 000 per centimetre. When light is shone through this grating, a pattern of interference fringes is seen.

We will firstly consider monochromatic light (light of a single wavelength). A laser can be used for this. The laser light is shone through the

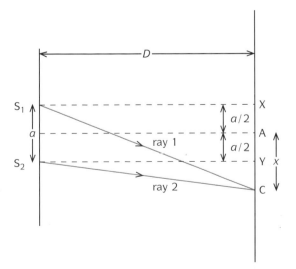

● *Figure 4.7* Construction for deriving $\lambda = ax/D$.

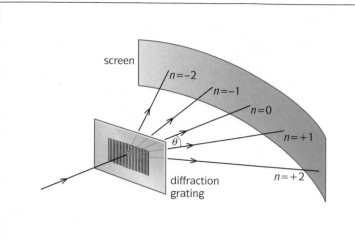

● **Figure 4.8** The diffracted beams form a symmetrical pattern on either side of the undiffracted central beam.

a

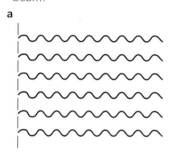

b

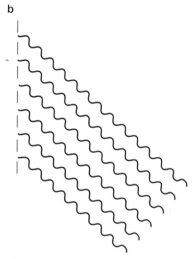

● **Figure 4.9**
**a** Waves from each slit are in step in the straight-through direction.
**b** In the direction of the first-order maximum, the waves are in step, but each has travelled one wavelength further than the one below it.

grating, at 90° to it. In the space beyond, interference fringes are formed. These can be observed on a screen, as with Young's slits. However, it is usual to measure the angle $\theta$ at which the fringes appear, rather than measuring their separation *(figure 4.8)*. (This is because, with Young's slits, the fringes are equally spaced and the angles are very small – recall the approximation used in deriving the equation $\lambda = ax/D$. With a diffraction grating, the angles are much larger and the fringes are not equally spaced.)

The fringes are referred to as maxima. The central fringe is called the zeroth-order maximum, the next fringe is the first-order maximum, and so on. The pattern is symmetrical, so there are two first-order maxima, two second-order maxima, etc.

## Explaining the experiment

The principle is the same as for the double-slit experiment, but here we have light passing through many slits. As it passes through each slit, it diffracts (spreads out) into the space beyond. So now we have many overlapping beams of light, and these interfere with one another. It is difficult to achieve constructive interference with many beams, because they all have to be in phase with one another.

There is a bright fringe, the zeroth-order maximum, in the straight-through direction ($\theta = 0$) because all of the rays here are travelling parallel to one another and in phase, so the interference is constructive *(figure 4.9a)*.

The first-order maximum forms as follows: rays of light emerge from all of the slits, and to form a bright fringe, all the rays must be in step. In the direction of the first-order maximum, ray 1 has travelled the least distance *(figure 4.9b)*. Ray 2 has travelled an extra distance equal to one wavelength and is therefore in step with ray 1. Ray 3 has travelled two extra wavelengths and is in step with rays 1 and 2. In fact, the rays from all of the slits are in step in this direction, and a bright fringe results.

### SAQ 4.6
Explain how the second-order maximum arises.

## Determining $\lambda$

By measuring the angles at which the maxima occur, we can find the wavelength of the light giving rise to them. The wavelength $\lambda$ is related to the angle $\theta$ by:

$$d \sin \theta = n\lambda \qquad (4.2)$$

where $d$ is the separation of the slits in the grating and $n$ (= 0, 1, 2, etc.) is the order of the maximum.

We shall now do an example. When a diffraction grating having 3000 slits per centimetre is used to diffract monochromatic light, the angular separation of the zeroth- and first-order maxima is found to be 10.0°. What is the wavelength of the light?

Firstly, we must calculate $d$. Since there are 3000 slits per centimetre, their separation must be $d = 1\,\text{cm}/3000 = 3.33 \times 10^{-4}\,\text{cm} = 3.33 \times 10^{-6}\,\text{m}$.

We also know that $\theta = 10.0°$ and $n = 1$. So, using *equation 4.2*, we have:

$$\lambda = \frac{d \sin \theta}{n} = \frac{3.33 \times 10^{-6}\,\text{m} \times \sin(10.0°)}{1}$$

$$= 580\,\text{nm}$$

## SAQ 4.7

**a** For the case described in the worked example above, at what angle would you expect to find the second-order maximum ($n=2$)? (Note that the answer is not 20°.)

**b** Repeat the calculation of $\theta$ for $n = 3, 4$, etc. What is the limit to this calculation? How many maxima will there be altogether in this interference pattern? (Remember to count the zeroth-order maximum, and those maxima for which $n$ is negative.)

## SAQ 4.8

Consider *equation 4.2*, $d \sin\theta = n\lambda$. How will the diffraction pattern change if:

**a** the wavelength of the light is increased;

**b** the diffraction grating is changed for one with slits that are spaced more closely?

## *The derivation of* $d \sin \theta = n\lambda$

This derivation is similar to that for Young's slits. However, in this case we are concerned with deducing the angles between adjacent bright fringes, rather than their separation on a screen. *Figure 4.10a* shows the origin of the zeroth-order ($n = 0$) maximum.

Parallel rays of light emerge from each slit, in phase with one another. Since they are parallel,

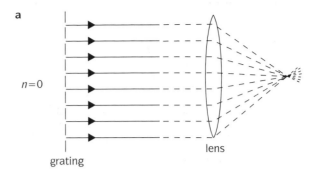

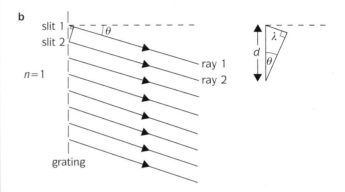

● *Figure 4.10* Construction for deriving $d \sin \theta = n\lambda$.

they remain in phase and give a bright fringe resulting from constructive interference. (You may think that if the rays are parallel, they will never meet and hence they will never interfere. You are right! However, in practice the rays are usually collected together by a lens, which focusses them to give a bright fringe. This might be a lens in a spectrometer or the lens in your eye, when you view the bright fringes.)

*Figure 4.10b* shows the origin of the first-order ($n = 1$) maximum. There is a path difference of $\lambda$ between rays from adjacent slits. We can see the extra distance travelled by ray 1 relative to ray 2 by drawing a line from slit 2, perpendicular to ray 1. This creates a small right-angled triangle, the short side of which is equal to the path difference. Once ray 1 has travelled this short extra distance, rays 1 and 2 continue in parallel and in step.

From the geometry of the situation, it is easy to see that the triangle has an angle $\theta$ opposite to the side of length $\lambda$, and it follows that:

$$\sin \theta = \frac{\lambda}{d} \quad \text{or} \quad d \sin \theta = \lambda$$

For the maximum of order $n$, the path difference between adjacent rays would be $n\lambda$, and we would have:

$$d \sin \theta = n\lambda$$

## Diffracting white light

A diffraction grating can be used to split white light up into its constituent colours (wavelengths). This is shown in *figure 4.11*. A beam of white light is shone onto the grating. A zeroth-order, white maximum is observed at $\theta = 0$, because all waves of each wavelength are in phase in this direction.

On either side, a series of spectra appears, with violet closest to the centre, and red furthest away. We can see why different wavelengths have their maxima at different angles if we rearrange the equation $d \sin \theta = n\lambda$:

$$\sin \theta = \frac{n\lambda}{d}$$

From this it follows that the greater the wavelength $\lambda$, the greater the value of $\sin \theta$ and hence the greater the angle $\theta$. Red light is at the long wavelength end of the visible spectrum, and so it appears at the greatest angle.

You can see similar effects in the light reflected from the surface of a compact disc. The disc has closely spaced tracks which form a spiral. Light reflected by the disc is diffracted by the regular pattern of tracks, and an interference pattern results.

Another interference effect is seen in the coloured fringes produced by light falling on a thin film of oil. Light is reflected from the top and bottom surfaces of the oil; interference between the two reflected beams of light gives rise to the colours that we see. The colour depends on both the thickness of the oil and the angle at which it is viewed.

### SAQ 4.9

White light is shone on to a diffraction grating with a slit separation $d$ of $2.00 \times 10^{-6}$ m. Calculate the angle between the red and violet ends of the first-order spectrum produced. (The visible spectrum has wavelengths between 400 nm and 700 nm.)

### SAQ 4.10

Explain why the second- and third-order spectra overlap.

## Practical measurements

A spectrometer (*figure 4.12*) is a laboratory instrument which uses a diffraction grating to split up light into its constituent wavelengths. Traditionally, a glass prism was used, but the calculation of

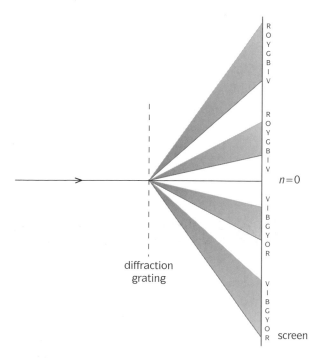

● *Figure 4.11* A diffraction grating is a simple way of dividing white light up into its constituent wavelengths.

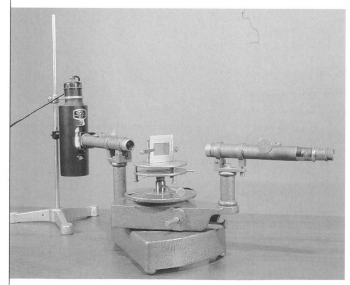

● *Figure 4.12* A spectrometer with a diffraction grating is used to determine the wavelengths present in visible light.

wavelengths is relatively complicated and requires a knowledge of the refractive index of the glass. Nowadays, diffraction gratings give good results, and allow wavelengths to be determined to a high degree of accuracy.

A simpler technique is shown in *figure 4.13*. You can use this arrangement to determine the wavelengths present in the light from a number of different sources. The viewer, looking through the diffraction grating, can see the sodium lamp directly. In addition, to either side, coloured images of the lamp can be seen. These are the first- and second-order maxima. Because only a few colours are seen, we can deduce that sodium light consists of only three or four visible wavelengths. The marker is moved along the half-metre rule until it coincides with the position of one of the images. The value of $\sin \theta$ can then be found, and

| Hydrogen | Sodium | Mercury | Helium |
|---|---|---|---|
| **656 red** | **589 yellow** | 579 yellow | 668 red |
| 486 blue–green | 569 yellow–green | 546 green | **588 yellow** |
| 434 blue | 420 violet | **436 blue** | 502 green |
| 410 violet | | 405 violet | 447 blue |

● **Table 4.1** The wavelengths (in nm) and colours present in the spectra of four elements; the most prominent wavelengths are shown in **bold**

hence $\lambda$ can be calculated. The process is repeated for each wavelength.

Note that in this experiment (or when using a spectrometer) it is best to measure the angle between, say, the two second-order maxima on either side of the straight-through position. This gives a large angle and hence reduces the uncertainty in $\theta$.

*Table 4.1* shows the most intense wavelengths present in the visible spectra of some typical lamps. Because different elements produce light of different wavelengths, it is possible to deduce the chemical composition of a substance by analysing the wavelengths present in its spectrum. This is the basis of the technique of optical spectrometry.

### SAQ 4.11

In an experiment with a diffraction grating, a student observes a strong red image of a hydrogen lamp ($\lambda = 656$ nm) at an angle of 25°. At what angle would she observe a strong yellow image of a sodium lamp ($\lambda = 589$ nm) using the same arrangement?

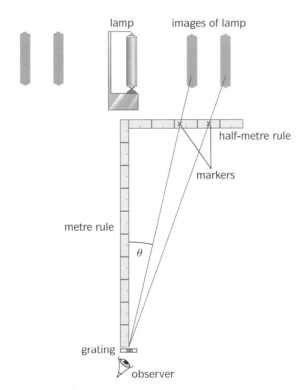

● **Figure 4.13** A laboratory arrangement equivalent to a spectrometer. The metre rule is lined up with the lamp. Coloured images are seen on either side. Markers are positioned on the half-metre rule, and the value of $\theta$ can then be found.

### SUMMARY

■ When light passes through a double slit, it is diffracted and an interference pattern of equally-spaced light and dark fringes is observed. This can be used to determine the wavelength of light, using $\lambda = ax/D$.

■ Light is also diffracted by a diffraction grating. The angle through which it is diffracted depends on the wavelength, and is given by $d \sin \theta = n\lambda$.

## Questions

1 Yellow sodium light of wavelength 589 nm is used in a double-slit experiment. The slit separation is 0.2 mm, and the screen is placed 1.20 m from the slits. What will be the separation of the fringes which appear on the screen?

2 A diffraction grating has equally spaced parallel slits, separated by $1.5 \times 10^{-6}$ m. Show that for red light (wavelength 700 nm) the grating gives maxima for values of $n$ up to 2. What is the highest-order maximum that will be produced for violet light (wavelength 400 nm)?

3 A student is trying to make an accurate measurement of the wavelength of green light from a mercury lamp ($\lambda = 546$ nm). Using a double slit of separation 0.5 mm, he finds he can see 10 clear fringes on a screen at a distance of 0.80 m from the slits. He can measure their overall width to within 1 mm.

   He then tries an alternative experiment using a diffraction grating that has 3000 lines per centimetre. He estimates that he can measure the angle between the second-order maxima to within 0.1°.

   a What will be the width of the 10 fringes that he can measure in the first experiment?

   b What will be the angle of the second-order maximum in the second experiment?

   c Discuss which experiment you think will give the more precise measurement of $\lambda$.

## Chapter five

# Electromagnetic waves

**By the end of this chapter you should be able to:**

1 describe the main features of the electromagnetic spectrum;

2 recall that all electromagnetic waves travel with the same speed in free space;

3 recall the orders of magnitude of the wavelengths of the principal radiations from radio waves to $\gamma$-rays;

4 recall and use the relationship:

intensity $\propto$ (amplitude)$^2$

## Light and electromagnetism

You are probably familiar with the idea that light is part of the electromagnetic spectrum; it is one of a family of electromagnetic wave phenomena. But it is not immediately obvious that light has any connection at all with electricity, magnetism and waves. These topics had been the subject of study by physicists for centuries before the connections between them became apparent.

Previously, we have looked at how electricity and magnetism are related. An electric current

● **Figure 5.1** The nineteenth century saw the birth of electromagnetic technology. This is a small section of a painting by Raoul Dufy that shows many of the pioneers of electrical science and engineering.

gives rise to a magnetic field; a changing magnetic field can cause a current to flow in an electrical conductor. These relationships led to the unification of the theories of electricity and magnetism by Michael Faraday in the mid-nineteenth century. A vast technology based on the theories of electromagnetism developed rapidly, and continues to expand today (*figure 5.1*).

### SAQ 5.1
What simple experiments show these relationships between electricity and magnetism? (These are covered in detail in chapters 8–11 of *Basic Physics 1 and 2*.)

## Electromagnetic radiation

Faraday's studies were extended by James Clerk Maxwell. He produced equations which showed that a changing electric or magnetic field would give rise to waves in space. When he calculated the speed of these waves, it turned out to be the known speed of light. He concluded that light is a wave in the form of a disturbance of the electric and magnetic fields in space.

Faraday had unified electricity and magnetism; now Maxwell had unified electromagnetism and light. By the end of the nineteenth century, more electromagnetic waves had been discovered:

■ radio waves, discovered by Heinrich Hertz, produced when a spark jumps through air;
■ infrared and ultraviolet waves, beyond the ends of the visible spectrum;
■ X-rays, discovered by Wilhelm Röntgen, produced when a beam of electrons collides with a metal target;
■ $\gamma$-rays, discovered by Henri Becquerel, produced by many radioactive substances.

We now regard all of these types of radiation as parts of the same electromagnetic spectrum, and we know that they can be produced in a variety of different ways.

## SAQ 5.2

We often refer to these types of radiation as electromagnetic waves. You are familiar with some experiments which show that light often behaves as a wave – it has wave-like properties. What properties are shared by all waves? (Wave properties have been dealt with in chapter 4 of *Basic Physics 1 and 2*.)

# The speed of light

Maxwell showed that the speed $c$ of electromagnetic radiation in free space was related to the permittivity of free space $\varepsilon_0$ and the permeability of free space $\mu_0$; the relationship is:

$$c^2 = \frac{1}{\mu_0 \varepsilon_0}$$

(You will recall that $\varepsilon_0$ appears in expressions for electric field strength, and $\mu_0$ appears in expressions for magnetic flux density.)

The constant $c$ is the speed at which all types of electromagnetic waves travel through free space (i.e. through a vacuum). If there is any matter present, the waves travel at a slower speed; they are no longer in free space.

## SAQ 5.3

In the SI system of units, the values of $c$ and $\mu_0$ are fixed:

$$c = 299\,792\,458\,\mathrm{m\,s^{-1}}$$

$$\mu_0 = 4\pi \times 10^{-7}\,\mathrm{H\,m^{-1}}$$

By substituting these values in Maxwell's equation for the speed of light, show that, in the SI system, the value of $\varepsilon_0$ is approximately $8.854 \times 10^{-12}\,\mathrm{F\,m^{-1}}$. What is the most precise value of $\varepsilon_0$ you can calculate with your calculator?

# Wavelengths and frequencies

All forms of electromagnetic radiation travel at the same speed $c$ in free space. It is useful to remember that the value of $c$ is given to a good approximation by:

$$c \simeq 3 \times 10^8\,\mathrm{m\,s^{-1}}$$

The wavelength $\lambda$ and frequency $f$ of the radiation are related to $c$ by:

$$c = f\lambda$$

If light travels from free space into a material

medium such as glass, its speed decreases but its frequency remains the same, and so we conclude that its wavelength must decrease. We often think of different forms of electromagnetic radiation as being characterised by their different wavelengths, but it might be better to think of their different frequencies as being their fundamental characteristic, since their wavelengths depend on the medium through which they are travelling.

## SAQ 5.4

Red light of wavelength 700 nm in free space passes into some glass, where its speed decreases to $2.0 \times 10^8\,\mathrm{m\,s^{-1}}$. Calculate:

a the frequency of the light in free space;

b its wavelength and frequency in the glass.

# Orders of magnitude

*Table 5.1* shows the approximate ranges of wavelengths (in free space) of the principal radiations which make up the electromagnetic spectrum. Some comments on the table follow.

■ There are no clear divisions between the different ranges in the spectrum; the divisions shown here are somewhat arbitrary.
■ Similarly, the naming of subdivisions is arbitrary. For example, microwaves are sometimes regarded as a subdivision of radio waves.
■ There is an overlap between the ranges of X-rays and γ-rays. The distinction is that X-rays are produced when electrons decelerate rapidly; γ-rays are produced by nuclear processes such as radioactive decay. However, there is no difference in the actual radiation between an X-ray and a γ-ray of wavelength, say, $10^{-11}\,\mathrm{m}$.
■ The spectrum is arranged here in order of decreasing wavelength. This corresponds to increasing frequency. It is sometimes referred to as increasing energy, since the energy of a photon of each type of radiation increases from radio waves (least energetic) to γ-rays (most energetic). (You should recall that the energy $E$ of a photon of electromagnetic radiation is related to the frequency $f$ of the radiation by $E = hf$, where $h$ is Planck's constant.)

| *Radiation* | *Wavelength range/m* | *Subdivisions* |
|---|---|---|
| radio waves | >$10^6$ to $10^{-1}$ | low frequency<br>medium frequency<br>high frequency<br>very high frequency (VHF)<br>ultra high frequency (UHF) |
| microwaves | $10^{-1}$ to $10^{-3}$ | |
| infrared | $10^{-3}$ to $7 \times 10^{-7}$ | far<br>intermediate<br>near |
| visible | $7 \times 10^{-7}$ to $4 \times 10^{-7}$ | ROYGBIV |
| ultraviolet | $4 \times 10^{-7}$ to $10^{-8}$ | |
| X-rays | $10^{-8}$ to $10^{-13}$ | soft<br>hard |
| $\gamma$-rays | $10^{-10}$ to $10^{-16}$ | |

● **Table 5.1** Wavelengths of the electromagnetic spectrum

● **Figure 5.2** The external aerial of this pocket television helps with the reception of waves in the VHF and UHF bands.

## SAQ 5.5

Copy *table 5.1*. Include an additional column showing the range of frequencies of each type of radiation.

## SAQ 5.6

Study *table 5.1* and answer the following questions.

a   Which type of radiation has the narrowest range of wavelengths?

b   Which has the second narrowest range?

c   By how many orders of magnitude do the ranges of X-rays and $\gamma$-rays overlap?

d   What is the range of wavelengths of microwaves, in millimetres?

e   What is the range of wavelengths of visible light, in nanometres?

f   What is the range of frequencies of visible light?

We use electromagnetic waves in many different ways. The wavelength must be chosen appropriately for each application. For example, X-rays are used to investigate the structure of materials: X-rays are diffracted as they pass between the planes of atoms which make up a crystal (their wavelength must be comparable to the spacing of atomic planes in order to achieve significant diffraction).

## SAQ 5.7

A pocket television has a telescopic aerial *(figure 5.2)*. When extended, this has a length of about 75 cm. Explain why this is useful for picking up VHF and UHF signals, which have wavelengths of up to 3 m, but does not enhance the reception of longer wavelength signals.

# The nature of electromagnetic waves

An electromagnetic wave is a disturbance in the electric and magnetic fields in space. *Figure 5.3* shows how we can represent such a wave. In this diagram, the wave is travelling from left to right.

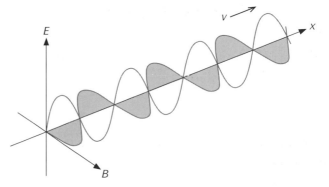

● **Figure 5.3** An electromagnetic wave is a periodic variation in electric and magnetic fields.

The electric field $E$ varies vertically, and the magnetic field $B$ varies horizontally. These are arbitrary choices; the point is that $E$ and $B$ vary at right angles both to one another and to the direction of travel of the wave.

An electromagnetic wave is **self-propagating** (it keeps itself going): the changing electric field causes the magnetic field to vary; the varying magnetic field causes the electric field to vary. Together, they result in the propagation of electromagnetic energy through space at the speed of light. Because electric and magnetic fields can exist in empty space, an electromagnetic wave does not need a medium to move through.

In electromagnetic waves, $E$ and $B$ vary at right angles to the direction of propagation, and hence they are described as transverse waves. We know that they are transverse because they can be polarised. For example, if light is passed through a piece of Polaroid, it becomes polarised. A second piece of Polaroid can be positioned so that it allows the light through (*figure 5.4a*); if it is rotated through 90°, the light is completely blocked (*figure 5.4b*). The first piece of Polaroid transmits only light with an electric field that varies vertically; the light which passes through is polarised in this direction, as shown by the action of the second piece of Polaroid.

Polarisation is a property of transverse waves only. A wave such as a sound wave is called a longitudinal wave; the particles of the medium through which the wave is travelling vibrate back-and-forth along the direction of propagation,

rather than at 90°. A longitudinal wave cannot be polarised because there is only one direction in which the vibrations can occur. In the case of a transverse wave, the vibrations can occur in any direction at 90° to the direction of propagation.

## Amplitude and intensity

The amplitude of a wave tells us the maximum variation from zero of the displacement which causes the wave. In the case of a water wave, the amplitude of the wave is the height of the wave crest above the undisturbed level of the water. For an electromagnetic wave, the amplitude is the greatest value of $E$ (or $B$).

Clearly, the amount of energy in a wave is related to the amplitude. The greater the amplitude, the greater is the energy carried by the wave. It turns out that the intensity of any wave (the rate at which it transmits energy) is proportional to the square of its amplitude:

$$\text{intensity} \propto (\text{amplitude})^2$$

Although a proof of this relationship is beyond the scope of this book, we will look at some examples which suggest that it is plausible.

The first example is shown in *figure 5.5*. This shows a water wave. In the second part of the diagram, it has the same wavelength as in the first part, but twice the amplitude. A wave like this has energy stored as potential energy. Since $E_p = mgh$, you should be familiar with the idea that $E_p$ depends on both the mass of the water and the height to which it has been raised. In the case of

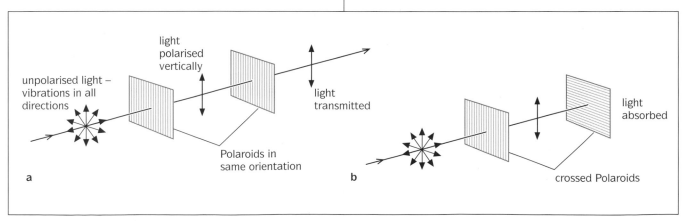

● *Figure 5.4* Light, initially unpolarised, becomes vertically polarised after passing through the first Polaroid. It is absorbed by a second Polaroid oriented at 90° to the first.

● *Figure 5.5* The second wave has double the amplitude of the first.

the wave with twice the amplitude, the mass of water raised has been doubled, and the average height to which it has been raised has also been doubled. Hence the potential energy stored is four times as much as that stored by the first wave.

For the second example, we will think about a mass on a spring performing simple harmonic motion *(figure 5.6)*. (All waves involve some kind of s.h.m., as discussed in chapter 4.) When it is at the limit of its oscillation, it has potential energy. This is stored in the stretched spring and is proportional to $x^2$, the square of the extension. Hence doubling the amplitude gives four times the stored energy. When the mass is at the midpoint of its oscillation, it has kinetic energy. If the amplitude is doubled, its speed is doubled. Since $E_k = {}^1\!/_2 mv^2$, it follows that doubling the amplitude doubles the speed and results in four times the kinetic energy.

It turns out that the relationship intensity ∝ (amplitude)$^2$ is true for all types of waves, including electromagnetic waves. The intensity of a beam of radiation is often measured as the rate of energy transfer per unit area. For example, the intensity of the Sun's radiation at the Earth's

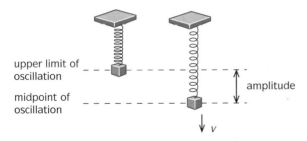

● *Figure 5.6* The energy of an oscillating mass–spring system is proportional to the square of the amplitude.

● *Figure 5.7* When the beam is broadened after passing through the two lenses, its intensity is reduced.

surface is about $1\,\mathrm{kW\,m^{-2}}$ when the Sun is directly overhead. In other words, about $1\,\mathrm{kW}\ (1000\,\mathrm{J\,s^{-1}})$ of energy falls on each $1\,\mathrm{m^2}$ of the Earth's surface.

### SAQ 5.8

The laser beam shown in *figure 5.7* passes through a pair of lenses and emerges with twice the diameter. Explain how the following change after the beam has passed through the lenses:

a  the area of the beam;

b  the amplitude of the light wave.

### SAQ 5.9

A laser produces a narrow beam of red light of intensity $10\,\mathrm{mW\,cm^{-2}}$; an X-ray machine produces a beam of X-rays of intensity $100\,\mathrm{W\,cm^{-2}}$.

a  Which has the greater wavelength?

b  What is the ratio of the amplitudes of the two waves?

## SUMMARY

■ The electromagnetic spectrum includes radio waves, microwaves, infrared, visible light, ultraviolet, X-rays and γ-rays (in order of decreasing wavelength).

■ All electromagnetic waves travel at the same speed $c$ in free space. This is referred to as the speed of light, and is given by:

$$c^2 = \frac{1}{\mu_0 \varepsilon_0}$$

where $\mu_0$ is the permeability of free space and $\varepsilon_0$ is the permittivity of free space.

■ The intensity of any wave is related to its amplitude by the relationship: intensity ∝ (amplitude)$^2$.

## Questions

1 For each of the following wavelengths (measured in free space), say what type of electromagnetic radiation it corresponds to: 1 km, 3 cm, 50 nm, 500 nm, 5000 nm, $10^{-12}$ m.

2 For each of the following frequencies, say what type of electromagnetic radiation it corresponds to: 200 kHz, 100 MHz, $5 \times 10^{14}$ Hz, $10^{18}$ Hz.

3 A crystal of quartz can be used as a diffraction grating for X-rays. Explain why this is so.

4 Sketch two waves, A and B, such that A has twice the wavelength and half the intensity of B.

## Chapter six

# Electrostatics

### By the end of this chapter you should be able to:

1 state that there are two types of charge, positive and negative;

2 describe and explain charging by friction and by induction, appreciating that charge is conserved;

3 describe an experiment which demonstrates that like charges repel and unlike charges attract;

4 distinguish between electrical conductors and insulators, and give typical examples;

5 use a simple electron model to distinguish between conductors and insulators;

6 describe simple practical applications of electrostatic phenomena, including paint spraying and dust extraction;

7 appreciate the potential hazards associated with charging by friction.

## Electric charge

You will be familiar with the idea of electric charge from your previous studies of static electricity, electric fields and electric current. However, it is hard to say precisely what electric charge is. It is a fundamental property of some microscopic particles (for example protons and electrons) which gives rise to a force between such particles. In this

● *Figure 6.1* Benjamin Franklin flew a kite during a thunderstorm to show that lightning is a form of electricity. This is a dangerous experiment, not to be copied.

chapter, we will develop further this microscopic picture of charge, and look at the macroscopic observations that first pointed towards the existence of this property.

Static electricity is observed in nature; lightning is the most striking example. This was investigated by Benjamin Franklin *(figure 6.1)* in a highly dangerous series of experiments, which involved flying a kite during a thunderstorm. He was able to show that sparks jumped to the ground, and that these were the same as the familiar sparks seen in experiments with electric current. Subsequently, two experimenters were killed while carrying out similar experiments, proving that water, electricity and ignorance don't mix.

## Charging up

There are several ways in which an object may be charged up.

### Charging by friction

In order to investigate static electricity, rods of different insulating materials may be charged by friction *(figure 6.2)*. One rod is suspended by an insulating thread so that it is free to turn. It is charged by rubbing with a woollen cloth or other piece of material. Then, when a second charged rod is brought close to the suspended rod, attraction or repulsion between them may be observed. (Another way to do this is to balance the rods on upturned watchglasses, so that they are free to turn.)

This experiment is somewhat unpredictable, for a variety of reasons.

■ Insulating rods are used so that they retain their charge. However, charge may leak away into the air, particularly on a damp day. It may also leak away up the suspension thread.

■ The nature of the charge acquired by a rod (positive or negative) depends both on the material of the rod and on the material with which it is rubbed.

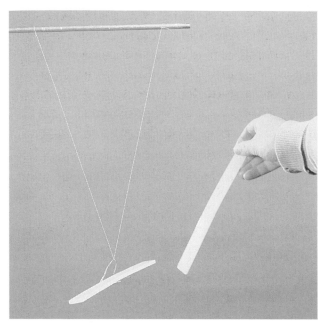

● **Figure 6.2** Investigating the attraction and repulsion between charged rods.

■ If the rod is handled carelessly, different regions may have different charges.

In early experiments, it was realised that there are two types of charge, which we now call positive and negative. It was arbitrarily decided to declare that glass becomes positively charged when rubbed with silk, and ebonite becomes negatively charged when rubbed with cat's fur. This choice was made long before the existence of electrons became known; a consequence has been that we talk of electric current flowing from positive to negative, whereas in most cases the current is formed by electrons flowing from negative to positive. If the decision had been to say that glass became negatively charged, we would not have this confusion. *Table 6.1* shows the type of charge acquired by different materials when rubbed with a woollen cloth.

| Materials acquiring positive charge | Materials acquiring negative charge |
|---|---|
| glass | polythene |
| acrylic (e.g. Perspex) | ebonite |
| | rubber |

● **Table 6.1** Responses of materials to rubbing with a woollen cloth

**SAQ 6.1**

A student investigated the attraction and repulsion between charged rods; the results are shown in *table 6.2*. Comment as fully as you can on these results.

| Rod 1 | Rod 2 | Observation |
|---|---|---|
| polythene | polythene | repulsion |
| polythene | Perspex | attraction |
| Perspex | Perspex | repulsion |
| glass | Perspex | repulsion |
| polythene | glass | attraction |
| ebonite | ebonite | attraction |
| ebonite | glass | attraction |

● **Table 6.2** Observations for SAQ 6.1

## Charging by induction

Another way in which an object can be charged is by induction. Here, a charged object is brought close to an uncharged one. There is a force of attraction between them. If the uncharged object is then touched, it may become permanently charged *(figure 6.3)*. In this way, an uncharged object may be attracted by a charged object; it is not possible for repulsion to be produced by electrostatic induction.

## Charging by contact

A third way to charge an object is by touching it with, or connecting it to, an object which is already charged. The charge is shared between the two objects. This method requires the objects to be made of materials with sufficient electrical conductivity for electrons to flow from one object to the other.

a charged rod is brought close to the sphere

the sphere is touched briefly before the rod is removed

metal sphere

insulating stand

● **Figure 6.3** Charging an object by electrostatic induction.

## Attraction and repulsion

Experiments with charged objects show the familiar rules governing the direction of the force between two charged objects:

like charges repel and unlike charges attract

In this context, the word 'like' means 'same', that is, both positive or both negative. 'Unlike' means 'different' or 'opposite', that is, one positive and one negative.

### SAQ 6.2

Compare the rules for like and unlike charges with:

a   the rules for forces between like and unlike magnetic poles;

b   the rules for forces between parallel and antiparallel electric currents.

# Explaining electrostatics

Because electrons are loosely bound on the outside of atoms, they are relatively free to move, and it is usually the movement of electrons which gives rise to the effects of electrostatics. In a neutral material, there are equal amounts of positive and negative charge. (In practice, this means that there are equal numbers of protons and electrons.)

In charging by friction, electrons are rubbed off one material on to the other, which thus gains a net negative charge. The material that has lost electrons is left with a net positive charge.

*Figure 6.4* shows how charges move during the process of charging by electrostatic induction. Object 1 is a good conductor and is initially neutral; object 2 is negatively charged *(figure 6.4a)*.

Electrons in 1 are repelled by 2 as 2 comes closer, leaving a positive charge close to 2 *(figure 6.4b)*. The two objects thus attract one another.

If 1 is now touched or otherwise connected to earth, the repelled electrons will flow away *(figure 6.4c)*. When the connection is removed, 1 is left with a net positive charge *(figure 6.4d)*. Hence a negatively charged object (2) has been used to give a neutral object (1) a positive charge.

Of course, the total amount of charge remains the same during any charging process: charge is conserved. (In our example, the negative charge is not destroyed – it has returned to earth.)

## Attracting an insulator

We have discussed how an electrical conductor can be charged by induction, but electrical insulators can also respond to the presence of a nearby charged object. You may have observed this if you have ever charged up a balloon by rubbing it – the balloon will stick to a wall or ceiling. This is another example of electrostatic induction.

An insulating material does not have electrons that are free to move throughout the bulk of the material. However, many insulating materials are made of polar molecules; such molecules are neutral overall, but they have regions of positive and negative charge. If a positively charged object is brought close to such a material, the molecules may rotate, bringing their negatively charged regions closer to the attracting object *(figure 6.5)*. We say that the material has become **polarised**.

When the charged object is removed, the molecules return to their original, random orientations.

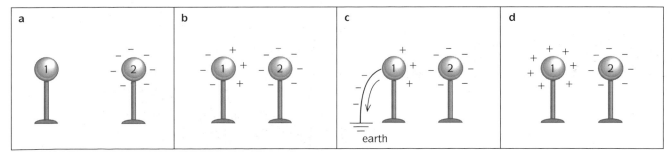

● **Figure 6.4** The movement of electric charge during charging by induction.

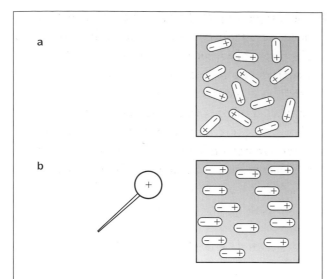

● **Figure 6.5**

**a** In a polar material, the molecules are oriented randomly.

**b** When a charged object is brought close, the molecules rotate. In this case, there is a net movement of negative charge towards the positively charged object, and the two now attract one another.

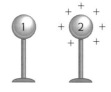

● **Figure 6.6** Charging by induction – how do the charges move?

● **Figure 6.7** Objects 1 and 2 are touching. If they are separated before 3 is removed, they retain their charges.

### SAQ 6.3

*Figure 6.6* shows the same initial situation as *figure 6.4a*, except that object 2 is positively charged. In this case, when 1 is touched, electrons flow from earth to the object. Draw a series of diagrams like those in *figure 6.4* to show how 1 becomes negatively charged.

### SAQ 6.4

*Figure 6.7* shows how two objects can be charged simultaneously by the process of induction. Write a paragraph to explain how this works.

# Conductors and insulators

You will be familiar with the idea that metals are good conductors of electricity and that, in general, non-metals are not. In the *Foundation Physics* module, you studied the idea of the resistivity $\rho$ of a material. By comparing the resistivities of different materials, we can see the great range of values that this property can have. *Table 6.3* shows some examples.

From *table 6.3*, you will see that resistivity has a great range of values. The best polymers (such as Perspex) are better insulators than the most conductive metals by a factor of $10^{23}$. The difference arises largely from the difference in the concentration of free electrons in the materials.

## Inside a metal

*Figure 6.8* shows how we picture the structure of a metal. When millions of neutral metal atoms combine together to form a piece of metal, their outermost electrons become detached. Usually about one electron breaks away from each atom. This leaves the atoms as positively charged ions, held together by the attraction of the free electrons. (This is metallic bonding.)

| Material | Resistivity $\rho/\Omega$m | Comment |
|---|---|---|
| silver | $1.5 \times 10^{-8}$ | the best conductor |
| copper | $1.6 \times 10^{-8}$ | cheaper than silver |
| gold | $2.0 \times 10^{-8}$ | used in electronic circuits |
| iron | $8.9 \times 10^{-8}$ | a typical metal |
| silicon | $10^2$ | a semiconductor |
| glass | $10^6$–$10^{12}$ | very variable – depends on composition |
| diamond | $10^{12}$ | a form of carbon |
| polymers | $10^8$–$10^{15}$ | good insulators |

● **Table 6.3** Resistivities of some solid materials, measured at room temperature

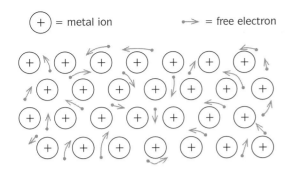

+ = metal ion → = free electron

● *Figure 6.8* In a metal, free electrons move around among a regular array of positively charged ions.

You may come across a variety of ways of describing these electrons. They are 'free electrons' (because they are relatively free to move about within the metal). They are also referred to as 'conduction electrons', because they take part in the processes of electrical and thermal conduction. You may also see the electrons referred to as a 'sea' of electrons, because we picture them 'washing about' inside the metal, carrying energy with them. They are also referred to as a 'gas' of electrons, because they bounce around inside the metal, rather like the molecules which make up a gas and which bounce around inside their container.

A semiconductor such as silicon has very few free electrons in it, perhaps only one for every $10^{10}$ atoms. A polymer is generally an insulating material, because all of the electrons are tied up in bonding within and between molecules. Polymers do conduct to a limited degree, but this is because of defects in their structure or composition, which release a very few free electrons.

## Some exceptions

As a general rule, metals are good electrical conductors while non-metals are good insulators. However, it is worth noting some exceptions.

■ Graphite is a form of carbon which conducts fairly well. The carbon atoms are arranged in planes, and there are some unbound electrons which can move freely within these planes.

■ Conducting polymers have been devised in which some electrons are free to move along the length of the polymer chains.

■ Some types of glass have been developed which have reasonable conductivity when heated. Here, it is often the case that ions, as well as electrons, are free to move. Such materials are used in fuel cells where the energy of a fuel is converted directly to electrical energy.

■ Wood is a poor conductor, but most types of wood are not sufficiently good insulators for use in electrostatics experiments. Charge tends to leak away – the conductivity arises from the presence of water in the wood.

## Comparing high resistivities

You can investigate the relative resistivities of different materials by comparing how well they serve to insulate a charged object. A suitable arrangement is shown in *figure 6.9*. A gold-leaf electroscope is charged by induction; the deflection of the gold leaf indicates the potential difference between it and the case. Position a wooden ruler so that it connects the plate of the electroscope to the bench. The leaf will gradually drop as the charge leaks away through the ruler. Repeat the experiment with a Perspex ruler, polythene and ebonite rods, and any other suitable materials.

### SAQ 6.5

Discuss the following points in relation to the experiment above.

**a** How could you use this experiment to compare the resistivities of different materials? (Make sure you take into account of the dimensions of the rulers and other factors.)

**b** If charge leaks away slowly into the atmosphere, what influence will this have on the results of the experiment?

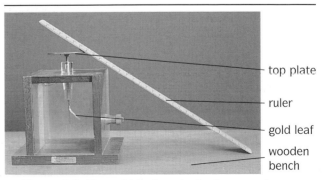

top plate

ruler

gold leaf

wooden bench

● *Figure 6.9* The gold leaf gradually drops as charge leaks away through the wooden ruler.

# Using electrostatics

There are many technological applications of electrostatics, and in particular of electrostatic induction. Here is a selection.

## *Electrostatic crop-spraying*

Many pests of crops live on the undersides of leaves where it is difficult to spray pesticides. Agricultural engineers have developed a technique for getting the spray to these awkward places *(figure 6.10)*. The nozzle of the spray is connected to a high voltage supply. This induces an opposite charge in the ground and in the plants which are being sprayed. Charged droplets are then attracted to both sides of the leaves.

## *Ink jet printing*

Many bottles and cans are now labelled on the production line to show their batch number, 'best before' date and so on. The print is made up of many tiny dots of ink. The ink droplets are charged up at a charge electrode, and then deflected by a steady electric field between deflector plates. Droplets are charged to different voltages so that they are deflected to different extents. Up to 2000 characters (letters and numbers) per second can be printed in this way on containers moving on a conveyor at $5\,\mathrm{m\,s^{-1}}$. Ink jet printers for computers work in a similar way.

## *Dust precipitation*

The gases emitted by chimneys, for example at power stations, contain dust and dirt particles, which must be removed to reduce the environmental damage that results from burning fuels. This can be done using electrostatic precipitators *(figure 6.11)*. A series of wires at high negative voltages (around $50\,\mathrm{kV}$) are mounted about $250\,\mathrm{mm}$ apart in the chimney. The electric field around these wires is very strong, and results in a corona discharge. Any free electrons in the air close to the wires are accelerated away; they collide with molecules in the air to cause further ionisation, and the result is an avalanche of electrons moving outwards from the wires. There is a blue glow around the wires.

Electrons and negative ions collide with dust particles, which thus acquire a negative charge. They are attracted towards the inner walls of the

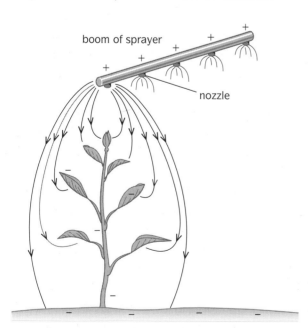

● *Figure 6.10* Electrostatics helps the pesticide spray reach the undersides of the leaves, targetting the pests and saving waste.

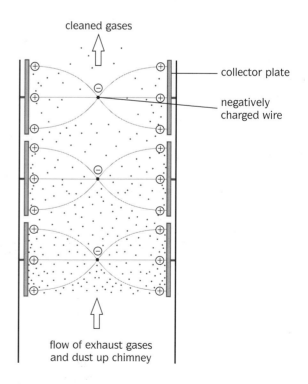

● *Figure 6.11* Electrostatic dust precipitators are fitted to power-station chimneys.

chimney, where they stick. Hammers strike the collector plates at regular intervals to dislodge the dust, which falls into hoppers below, ready for collection and disposal.

## SAQ 6.6

Consider the three examples of the use of electrostatics described above. In which of these examples does electrostatic induction play a part?

## SAQ 6.7

Electrostatics is also made use of in paint spraying, for example in painting car body panels. Particles of resinous paint are sprayed on to the panel, and it is then baked in an oven. *Figure 6.12* shows how this is done.

**a** Use this diagram to explain the process.

**b** Explain why this gives a better covering of paint.

**c** Explain why this technique is less wasteful of paint.

# Static hazards

Electrostatics has its uses, but it can also be hazardous. You will have experienced the sort of electric shock that can arise when you walk on certain types of carpet, or from sitting on some car seats. When you touch a door handle or the metal car body, a spark jumps between you and the earthed metal. Friction between your feet and the carpet, or between your clothing and the car seat, has given you an electric charge – you may be charged up to many kilovolts. This can be a minor discomfort, but it can also be a serious problem. Discharge sparks can interfere with computers, and

● **Figure 6.13** Before fuel is pumped into this aircraft, it is connected to the tanker by a conducting cable (seen here enclosed in striped tape, on the left) to reduce the danger of sparks.

many computer installations are fitted with special carpets made from fabric that conducts away any build-up of charge.

Friction can also give rise to unwanted static charges when fuel such as petrol flows along a pipeline. This is a problem when aircraft are being refuelled, and when petrol stations are being restocked from a tanker. A conducting cable must be connected between the aircraft (or the petrol station storage tanks) and the fuel tanker (*figure 6.13*), to ensure that the static charge is shared equally between them. Then there will be no chance of a spark which could ignite the fuel.

Similarly, ocean-going oil tankers have a problem, because their tanks may well contain a fuel–air mixture that could easily be ignited by any small spark. Sailors are required to wear conducting shoes, to ensure that they do not build up static charge as they walk around the ship. Problems can also arise when the tanks are sprayed with jets of water to remove sediment. The water droplets may become charged, and sparks could result. To reduce the danger of explosion, the fuel–air mixture in the empty tanks is replaced by an inert atmosphere of exhaust gases from the ship's engines.

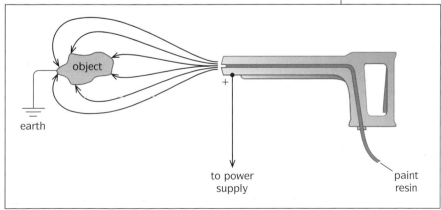

● **Figure 6.12** Electrostatics can help with paint spraying.

A+   C−
B+

## SAQ 6.8

Explain how the wearing of conducting shoes by sailors can reduce the danger of explosions on board an oil tanker.

## SAQ 6.9

Are human beings conductors or insulators? Explain your answer.

---

# SUMMARY

- There are two types of electric charge: positive and negative.

- Like charges repel and unlike charges attract. This can be shown by simple experiments involving charged rods of different materials.

- There are several methods for charging an object: by friction, by induction (bringing another charged object nearby), or by contact with another charged object.

- In an electrical conductor, there are free electrons which are able to move throughout the material; in an insulator, there are very few free electrons.

- There are many technological applications of electrostatics, including electrostatic crop-spraying, ink jet printing, dust precipitation and paint spraying.

- The sparks that can result from charging by friction may be hazardous.

---

# Questions

1 *Figure 6.14* shows the results of an experiment in electrostatics using three charged objects. Object A repels B but attracts C. What can you deduce about:
   a  the charges on A and B;
   b  the charges on A and C;
   c  the effect of bringing B close to C?

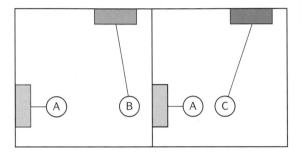

● *Figure 6.14*  An experiment in electrostatics.

2 a  Explain why a good electrical conductor is also a good thermal conductor.
   b  Some good electrical insulators are poor thermal insulators. Why is this?

3 a  If you rub a plastic ruler on a woollen jumper, you can use it to attract a stream of water from a tap. Explain this observation.
   b  Why will this experiment not work using a metal ruler?

4  A plastic comb is rubbed with a cloth. It is then found to attract a small piece of paper, which sticks to the comb. Shortly after, the paper jumps off the comb. Explain these observations, referring to the movement of charged particles.

## Chapter seven

# Capacitors

**By the end of this chapter you should be able to:**

1 derive and use formulae for capacitors in series and in parallel;

2 use the area under the potential–charge graph to derive the equation for energy stored:

$$W = \frac{1}{2} QV = \frac{1}{2} CV^2$$

## Capacitors in parallel

Capacitors are used in electric circuits to store charge and energy. Situations often arise where two or more capacitors are connected together in a circuit. In this section, we will look at capacitors connected in parallel. The next section deals with capacitors in series.

When two capacitors are connected in parallel (*figure 7.1*), their combined capacitance is simply the sum of their individual capacitances:

$$C_{total} = C_1 + C_2 \qquad (7.1)$$

This is because, when the two capacitors are connected together, they are equivalent to a single capacitor with larger plates. The bigger the plates, the more the charge that can be stored for a given voltage, and hence the greater the capacitance.

The charge $Q$ stored by the two capacitors connected in parallel and charged to a potential difference $V$ is simply given by:

$$Q = C_{total} \times V \qquad (7.2)$$

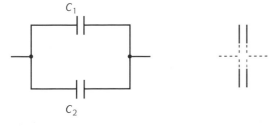

● **Figure 7.1** Two capacitors connected in parallel are equivalent to a single, larger capacitor.

*SAQ 7.1*

**a** Calculate the capacitance of two $100\,\mu\text{F}$ capacitors connected in parallel.

**b** Calculate the charge they store when charged to a p.d. of 20 V.

### Deriving the formula

We can derive *equation 7.1* by thinking about the charge stored by the two capacitors. As shown in *figure 7.2*, $C_1$ stores charge $Q_1$ and $C_2$ stores charge $Q_2$. Since the p.d. across each capacitor is $V$, we can write:

$$Q_1 = C_1 V \quad \text{and} \quad Q_2 = C_2 V$$

The total charge stored is given by the sum of these:

$$Q = Q_1 + Q_2 = C_1 V + C_2 V$$

Since $V$ is a common factor:

$$Q = (C_1 + C_2)\,V$$

Comparing this with $Q = C_{total}\,V$ gives the required $C_{total} = C_1 + C_2$. It follows that for three or more capacitors connected in parallel, we have:

$$C_{total} = C_1 + C_2 + C_3 + \ldots$$

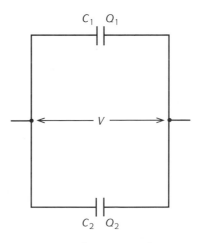

● **Figure 7.2** Two capacitors connected in parallel have the same p.d. across them, but store different amounts of charge.

### SAQ 7.2

Consider two capacitors, $C_1 = 200\,\mu F$ and $C_2 = 500\,\mu F$, charged up to a p.d. of 10 V. Following the steps of the argument above, calculate the charge stored by each individually and the total charge they store, and hence show that their combined capacitance when connected in parallel is 700 μF.

### SAQ 7.3

A capacitor of value 50 μF is required, but the only values available to you are 10 μF, 20 μF and 100 μF. How would you achieve the required value?

## Capacitors in series

In a similar way to the case of capacitors connected in parallel, we can consider two or more capacitors connected in series *(figure 7.3)*. The combined capacitance of $C_1$ and $C_2$ is given by:

$$\frac{1}{C_{total}} = \frac{1}{C_1} + \frac{1}{C_2} \qquad (7.3)$$

Here, it is the reciprocals of the capacitances which must be added to give the reciprocal of the total capacitance. For three or more capacitors connected in series, we have:

$$\frac{1}{C_{total}} = \frac{1}{C_1} + \frac{1}{C_2} + \frac{1}{C_3} + \dots$$

The following example shows the way in which these equations work. Calculate the combined capacitance of a 300 μF capacitor and a 600 μF capacitor connected in series.

The calculation should be done in two steps; this is relatively simple using a calculator with a '1/x' key. Substituting the values in *equation 7.3* gives:

$$\frac{1}{C_{total}} = \frac{1}{C_1} + \frac{1}{C_2} = \frac{1}{300\,\mu F} + \frac{1}{600\,\mu F}$$

$$= \frac{1}{200\,\mu F}$$

Now take the reciprocals of both sides:

$$C_{total} = 200\,\mu F$$

● *Figure 7.3* Two capacitors connected in series.

Notice that the combined capacitance of the two capacitors in series is less than either of the individual capacitances.

### SAQ 7.4

Calculate the combined capacitance of three capacitors, 200 μF, 300 μF and 600 μF, connected in series.

### SAQ 7.5

a  What is significant about the combined capacitance of two *equal* capacitors connected in series? And of three equal capacitors in series?

b  What is significant about the combined capacitance of two or more equal capacitors connected in parallel?

### *Deriving the formula*

This follows the same principles as for the case of capacitors in parallel. *Figure 7.4* shows the situation. $C_1$ and $C_2$ are connected in series, and there is a p.d. $V$ across them. This p.d. is divided (it is shared between the two capacitors), so that the p.d. across $C_1$ is $V_1$ and the p.d. across $C_2$ is $V_2$. It follows that:

$$V = V_1 + V_2$$

Now we must think about the charge stored by the combination of capacitors. In *figure 7.4*, you

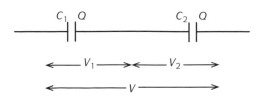

● *Figure 7.4* Capacitors connected in series store the same charge, but they have different p.d.s across them.

will see that both capacitors are shown as storing the same charge $Q$. How does this come about? When the voltage is first applied, charge $+Q$ arrives on the left-hand plate of $C_1$. This repels charge $+Q$ off the right-hand plate, leaving it with charge $-Q$. Charge $+Q$ now arrives on the left-hand plate of $C_2$, and this in turn results in charge $-Q$ on the right-hand plate.

Note that charge is not arbitrarily created or destroyed in this process – the total amount of charge in the system is constant. This is an example of the conservation of charge.

Notice also that there is a central isolated section of the circuit between the two capacitors. Since this is initially uncharged, it must remain so at the end. This requirement is satisfied, because there is charge $-Q$ at one end and $+Q$ at the other. Hence we conclude that capacitors connected in series store the same charge. This allows us to write equations for $V_1$ and $V_2$:

$$V_1 = \frac{Q}{C_1} \quad \text{and} \quad V_2 = \frac{Q}{C_2}$$

The combination of capacitors stores charge $Q$ when charged to p.d. $V$, and so we can write:

$$V = \frac{Q}{C_{\text{total}}}$$

Substituting these in $V = V_1 + V_2$ gives:

$$\frac{Q}{C_{\text{total}}} = \frac{Q}{C_1} + \frac{Q}{C_2}$$

Cancelling the common factor of $Q$ gives the required equation:

$$\frac{1}{C_{\text{total}}} = \frac{1}{C_1} + \frac{1}{C_2}$$

## The comparison with resistors

It is helpful to compare the formulae for capacitors in series and parallel with the corresponding formulae for resistors (*table 7.1*).

Notice that the reciprocal formula applies to capacitors in series but to resistors in parallel. This comes from the definitions of capacitance and resistance. Capacitance tells us how good a capacitor is at storing charge for a given voltage, and resistance tells us how bad a resistor is at letting current through for a given voltage.

### SAQ 7.6

The conductance $G$ of a resistor tells us how *good* a resistor is at letting current through for a given voltage. It is the reciprocal of the resistance: $G = 1/R$. Write down equations for the combined conductance $G_{\text{total}}$ of two resistors whose conductances are $G_1$ and $G_2$, connected **a** in series and **b** in parallel.

## Capacitor networks

There are four ways in which three capacitors may be connected together. These are shown in *figure 7.5*. The combined capacitance of the first two arrangements (three capacitors in series, three in parallel) can be calculated using the formulae above. The other combinations must be dealt with as follows:

| | Capacitors | Resistors |
|---|---|---|
| in series | $C_1$  $C_2$  $C_3$ <br> store same charge <br><br> $\frac{1}{C_{\text{total}}} = \frac{1}{C_1} + \frac{1}{C_2} + \frac{1}{C_3} + \ldots$ | $R_1$  $R_2$  $R_3$ <br> have same current <br><br> $R_{\text{total}} = R_1 + R_2 + R_3 + \ldots$ |
| in parallel | $C_1$ <br> $C_2$ <br> $C_3$ <br> have same p.d. <br><br> $C_{\text{total}} = C_1 + C_2 + C_3 + \ldots$ | $R_1$ <br> $R_2$ <br> $R_3$ <br> have same p.d. <br><br> $\frac{1}{R_{\text{total}}} = \frac{1}{R_1} + \frac{1}{R_2} + \frac{1}{R_3} + \ldots$ |

● *Table 7.1*

**a**

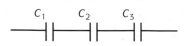

**b**

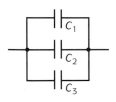

**c**

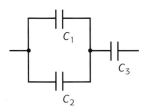

**d**

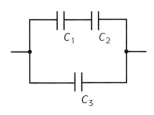

● **Figure 7.5** Four ways to connect three capacitors.

■ *Figure 7.5c*
Calculate $C_{total}$ for the two capacitors $C_1$ and $C_2$, which are connected in parallel, and then take account of the third capacitor $C_3$, which is connected in series.

■ *Figure 7.5d*
Calculate $C_{total}$ for the two capacitors $C_1$ and $C_2$, which are connected in series, and then take account of the third capacitor $C_3$, which is connected in parallel.

These are the same approaches as would be used for networks of resistors.

## SAQ 7.7

For each of the four circuits shown in *figure 7.5*, calculate the combined capacitance if each capacitor has a value of 100 μF.

## SAQ 7.8

Given a number of 100 μF capacitors, how might you connect networks to give the following values of capacitance:

**a** 400 μF;

**b** 25 μF;

**c** 250 μF?

# Stored energy

Capacitors are useful in electrical circuits because they store energy as well as charge. The energy $W$ stored by a capacitor $C$ charged to a p.d. $V$ is given by

$$W = \frac{1}{2}CV^2$$

(See *Basic Physics 1 and 2*, page 50.) The energy stored is proportional to the capacitance and to the square of the potential difference.

## *Deriving the formula*

In order to charge up a capacitor, work must be done to push the charge on to its plates (*figure 7.6*). At first, there is only a small amount of positive charge on the left-hand plate. Adding more charge is relatively easy, because there is not much repulsion. As the charge stored increases, the repulsion between the charge on the plate and the new charge increases, and a greater amount of work must be done to increase the charge stored.

This can be seen quantitatively in *figure 7.7a*. This graph shows how the p.d. $V$ increases as the amount of charge stored $Q$

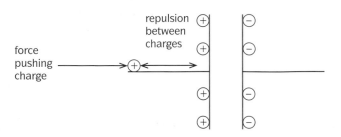

● **Figure 7.6** When a capacitor is charged, work must be done to push additional charge against the repulsion of the existing charge.

**a**

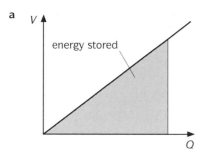

energy stored

**b**

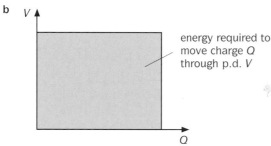

energy required to move charge $Q$ through p.d. $V$

● **Figure 7.7** The area under a current–charge graph gives a quantity of energy. The area in **a** shows the energy stored in a capacitor; the area in **b** shows the energy required to drive a charge through a p.d.

increases. It is a straight line because $Q$ and $V$ are related by:

$$V = \frac{Q}{C}$$

We can use this graph to calculate the work done in charging up the capacitor.

First, consider the work done $W$ in moving charge $Q$ through a p.d. $V$. This is given by:

$$W = QV$$

(You studied this equation in the *Foundation Physics* module.) From the graph of $Q$ against $V$ (*figure 7.7b*), we can see that the quantity $Q \times V$ is given by the area under the graph. If we apply the same idea to the capacitor graph (*figure 7.7a*), then the area under the graph is the shaded triangle, with an area of $^1/_2$ base × height. Hence the work done in charging a capacitor to a particular p.d. is given by:

$$W = \frac{1}{2}QV$$

Substituting $Q = CV$ into this equation gives:

$$W = \frac{1}{2}CV^2$$

This tells us the work done in charging up the capacitor. This is equal to the energy stored by the capacitor, since this is the amount of energy released when the capacitor is discharged.

**SAQ 7.9**

What is the gradient of the straight line shown in *figure 7.7a*?

**SAQ 7.10**

The graph of *figure 7.8* shows how $V$ depends on $Q$ for a particular capacitor. The area under the graph has been divided into strips to make it easy to calculate the energy stored. The first strip (which is simply a triangle) shows the energy stored when the capacitor is charged up to 1 V. The energy stored is $\frac{1}{2}QV = \frac{1}{2} \times 1\,\text{mC} \times 1\,\text{V} = 0.5\,\text{mJ}$.

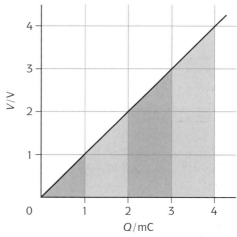

● **Figure 7.8** The energy stored by a capacitor is equal to the area under the charge–voltage graph.

**a** Copy the *table* and complete it by calculating the areas of successive strips, to show how $W$ depends on $V$.

**b** Plot a graph of $W$ against $V$. What shape does it have?

**c** What is the value of the capacitance $C$?

| $Q$/mC | $V$/V | Area of strip $\Delta W$/mJ | Sum of areas $W$/mJ |
|---|---|---|---|
| 1 | 1 | 0.5 | 0.5 |
| 2 | 2 | 1.5 | 2.0 |
| 3 | | | |
| 4 | | | |

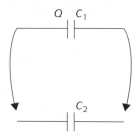

● **Figure 7.9** Capacitor $C_1$ is charged up and then connected across $C_2$.

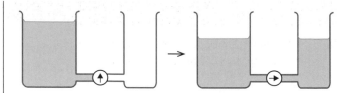

● **Figure 7.10** An analogy for the sharing of charge between capacitors.

## Sharing charge, sharing energy

If a capacitor is charged up and then connected to a second capacitor (*figure 7.9*), what happens to the charge and the energy which it stores? Note that when the capacitors are connected together, they are in parallel, because they have the same p.d. across them. Their combined capacitance $C_{total}$ is equal to the sum of their individual capacitances. Now we can think about the charge stored $Q$. This is shared between the two capacitors; the total amount of charge stored must remain the same, since charge is conserved. It is shared between the two capacitors in proportion to their capacitances. Now the p.d. can be calculated from $V = Q/C$, and the energy from $W = \frac{1}{2}CV^2$.

If we look at a numerical example, we find an interesting result. Consider two 100 mF capacitors. One is charged to 10 V, disconnected from the power supply, and then connected across the other. Initially we have:

> charge stored $Q = 100\,\text{mF} \times 10\,\text{V} = 1000\,\text{mC}$
> energy stored $W = \frac{1}{2}CV^2$
> $\qquad\qquad = \frac{1}{2} \times 100\,\text{mF} \times (10\,\text{V})^2$
> $\qquad\qquad = 5000\,\text{mJ}$

After connecting together, we have:

> combined capacitance $C_{total} = 200\,\text{mF}$
> charge stored $= 1000\,\text{mC}$
> p.d. $= \dfrac{1000\,\text{mC}}{200\,\text{mF}} = 5\,\text{V}$
> energy stored $= \frac{1}{2} \times 200\,\text{mF} \times (5\,\text{V})^2 = 2500\,\text{mJ}$

So, although the charge stored remains the same, the energy stored has fallen to half of its original value. When the capacitors are connected together, a current flows in the connecting wires, and energy is dissipated in overcoming their resistance. Energy is also dissipated as the current tends to oscillate back and forth in the wires, generating electromagnetic waves.

*Figure 7.10* shows an analogy to this situation. Capacitors are represented by containers of water. A wide (high capacitance) container is filled to a certain level (p.d.). It is then connected to a container with a smaller capacitance, and the levels equalise. (The p.d. is the same for each.) Notice that the potential energy of the water has decreased, because the height of its centre of gravity above the base level has decreased. Energy is dissipated as heat, as there is friction both within the moving water and between the water and the container.

### SAQ 7.11

A 20 μF capacitor is charged up to 200 V and then disconnected from the supply. It is then connected to a 5 μF capacitor. Calculate:

**a** their combined capacitance;

**b** the charge they store;

**c** the p.d. across the combination;

**d** the energy dissipated when they are connected together.

### SAQ 7.12

Draw a 'water container' diagram similar to that shown in *figure 7.10* to represent two capacitors of equal capacitance. One is filled to a high level, and then connected to the other.

**a** What is the final level of the water?

**b** What does this correspond to in the case of capacitors?

# SUMMARY

- For capacitors connected in series and in parallel, the combined capacitances are as follows:

In parallel:

$$C_{total} = C_1 + C_2 + C_3 + \ldots$$

In series:

$$\frac{1}{C_{total}} = \frac{1}{C_1} + \frac{1}{C_2} + \frac{1}{C_3} + \ldots$$

- The energy stored by a capacitor is equal to the area under the potential–charge graph, and is given by:

$$W = \tfrac{1}{2}QV \quad \text{or} \quad W = \tfrac{1}{2}CV^2$$

# Questions

1 You have three capacitors whose values are 100 pF, 200 pF and 600 pF. What are the greatest and least values of capacitance that you can make by connecting them together to form a network? How should they be connected in each case?

2 What is the capacitance of the network of capacitors shown in *figure 7.11*?

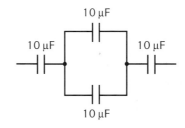

● **Figure 7.11** A capacitor network.

3 Three capacitors, each of capacitance 120 μF, are connected together in series. They are then connected to a 10 kV supply.
a What is their combined capacitance?
b How much charge do they store?
c How much energy do they store?

4 In a photographic flashgun, a 0.2 F capacitor is charged by a 9 V battery. It is then discharged in a flash of duration 0.01 s. Calculate:
a the charge and energy stored by the capacitor;
b the average power dissipated during the flash;
c the average current in the flash bulb;
d the approximate resistance of the bulb.

# Direct-current circuits

You are already able to solve many problems involving electrical circuits. In solving these, you make use of some important ideas: components in series have the same current flowing through them, components in parallel have the same p.d. across them, and so on. In this chapter, we will look at the formal statements of these ideas, and see how they can be used to solve problems in a variety of situations.

## Kirchhoff's first law

You have already come across this law in the *Foundation Physics* module. It states that:

The sum of the currents flowing into any point in a circuit is equal to the sum of the currents flowing out of that point.

This is illustrated in *figure 8.1*. In the first part of the figure, the current into point P must equal the current out, so:

$$I_1 = I_2$$

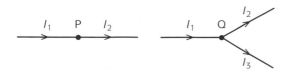

● **Figure 8.1** Kirchhoff's first law: conservation of current.

In the second part, we have one current flowing into point Q, and two currents flowing out. The current divides at Q. Kirchhoff's first law gives:

$$I_1 = I_2 + I_3$$

Kirchhoff's first law can thus be seen as a law of conservation of current. It can also be seen as a law of conservation of charge. It is impossible for charge to flow into a point in a circuit and not flow out again.

### SAQ 8.1

Use Kirchhoff's first law to deduce the value of $I_x$ in *figure 8.2*.

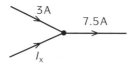

● **Figure 8.2**

### SAQ 8.2

In *figure 8.3*, how much current flows in wire X? In which direction does it flow (towards P or away from P)?

● **Figure 8.3**

## Kirchhoff's second law

This law deals with voltages in a circuit. We will start by considering a simple circuit which contains a battery and two resistors *(figure 8.4)*. Since this is a simple series circuit, the current $I$ must be the same all the way around, and we need not concern ourselves further with Kirchhoff's first law.

In this circuit, the e.m.f. of the battery provides the 'push' to make the current flow through the

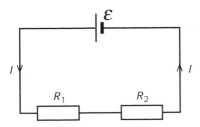

● **Figure 8.4** A simple series circuit.

resistors. Hence we can write:

$$\mathcal{E} = IR_1 + IR_2$$

e.m.f. of battery = sum of p.d.s across the resistors

You should not find these equations surprising. However, you may not realise that they are a consequence of applying Kirchhoff's second law to the circuit. This law states that:

The sum of the e.m.f.s around any loop in a circuit is equal to the sum of the p.d.s around the loop.

We shall look at another example of how this law can be applied, and then look at how it can be applied in general.

*Figure 8.5* shows a circuit with two batteries (connected back-to-front) and two resistors. Again, the current is the same all the way round the circuit. Using Kirchhoff's second law, we can find the value of *I*. First, we calculate the sum of the e.m.f.s, taking account of the way that the batteries are connected together:

sum of e.m.f.s = 6 V − 2 V = 4 V

Second, we calculate the sum of the p.d.s:

sum of p.d.s = $I \times 10\,\Omega + I \times 30\,\Omega = I \times 40\,\Omega$

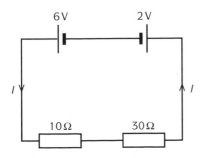

● **Figure 8.5** A circuit with two opposing batteries.

Equating these gives:

$$4\,V = I \times 40\,\Omega$$

and so $I = 0.1\,A$. No doubt, you could have solved this problem without formally applying Kirchhoff's second law.

# Applying Kirchhoff's laws

*Figure 8.6* shows a more complex circuit, with two 'loops'. Again there are two batteries and two resistors. The problem is to find the current flowing through the resistors. There are several steps in this.

1 Mark on the currents flowing. The diagram shows $I_1$, $I_2$ and $I_3$; note that it doesn't matter if we mark these flowing in the wrong directions, as they will simply appear as negative quantities in the solutions.

2 Apply Kirchhoff's first law. At point P, this gives:

$$I_1 + I_2 = I_3 \tag{1}$$

3 Choose a loop and apply Kirchhoff's second law. Around the upper loop, this gives:

$$6\,V = I_3 \times 30\,\Omega + I_1 \times 10\,\Omega \tag{2}$$

4 Repeat step 3 around other loops until there is the same number of equations as unknown currents. Around the lower loop, this gives:

$$2\,V = I_3 \times 30\,\Omega \tag{3}$$

We now have three equations with three unknowns (the three currents).

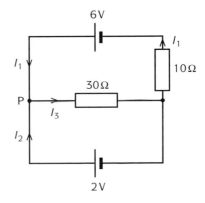

● **Figure 8.6** Kirchhoff's laws are needed to deduce the currents flowing in this circuit.

5 Solve these equations as simultaneous equations. In this case, the situation has been chosen to give simple solutions. *Equation 3* gives $I_3 = 0.067\,A$, and substituting this value in *equation 2* gives $I_1 = 0.4\,A$. We can now find $I_2$ by substituting in *equation 1*:

$$I_2 = I_3 - I_1 = 0.067\,A - 0.4\,A = -0.33\,A$$

Thus $I_2$ is negative – it flows in the opposite direction to the arrows shown in *figure 8.6*.

Note that there is a third 'loop' in this circuit; we could have applied Kirchhoff's second law to the outermost loop of the circuit. This gives a fourth equation:

$$6\,V - 2\,V = I_1 \times 10\,\Omega$$

However, this is not an independent equation; we could have arrived at it by subtracting *equation 3* from *equation 2*.

## Signs and directions

Caution is necessary when applying Kirchhoff's second law: you need to take account of the ways in which the sources of e.m.f. are connected, and the directions in which the currents are flowing. *Figure 8.7* shows a loop from a complicated circuit to illustrate this point. Only the components and currents within the loop are shown.

■ *E.m.f.s*
Starting with the cell $\mathcal{E}_1$ and working anticlockwise around the loop (because $\mathcal{E}_1$ is pushing current anticlockwise):

$$\text{sum of e.m.f.s} = \mathcal{E}_1 + \mathcal{E}_2 - \mathcal{E}_3$$

(Note that $\mathcal{E}_3$ is opposing the other two e.m.f.s.)

■ *P.d.s*
Starting from the same point, and working anticlockwise again:

$$\text{sum of p.d.s} = I_1R_1 - I_2R_2 - I_2R_3 + I_1R_4$$

(Note that $I_2$ is flowing clockwise, so the p.d.s that involve $I_2$ are negative.)

### SAQ 8.3

You can use Kirchhoff's second law to find the current $I$ flowing in the circuit shown in *figure 8.8*. Choosing the best loop can simplify the problem.

a   Which loop in the circuit should you consider?

b   What is the value of $I$?

### SAQ 8.4

Use Kirchhoff's second law to deduce the value of the resistor $R$ shown in the circuit loop of *figure 8.9*.

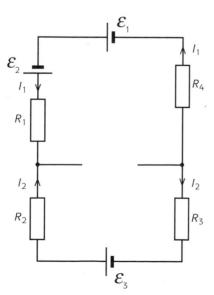

● **Figure 8.7** A loop extracted from a more complicated circuit.

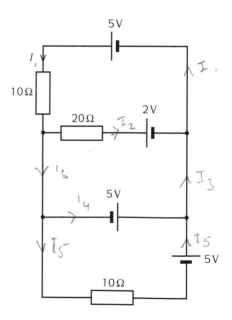

● **Figure 8.8** Careful choice of a suitable loop can make it easier to solve problems like this.

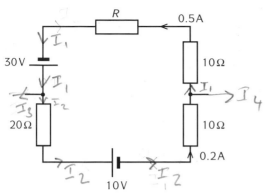

● **Figure 8.9** Find the value of *R*.

## Conservation of energy

Kirchhoff's second law is a consequence of the principle of conservation of energy. If a charge, say 1 C, moves around the circuit, it gains energy as it moves through each source of e.m.f. and loses energy as it passes through each p.d. If the charge moves all the way round the circuit, so that it ends up where it started, it must have the same energy at the end as at the beginning. (Otherwise we would be able to create energy from nothing simply by moving charges around circuits.) So:

energy gained passing through e.m.f.s
   = energy lost passing through p.d.s.

You should recall that an e.m.f. in volts is simply the energy gained by 1 C of charge as it passes through. Similarly, a p.d. is the energy lost by 1 C as it passes through. (1 volt = 1 joule per coulomb.) Hence we can think of Kirchhoff's second law as:

energy gained per coulomb around loop
   = energy lost per coulomb around loop

### SAQ 8.5

Use the idea of the energy gained and lost by a 1 C charge to explain why two 6 V batteries connected together in series can give an e.m.f. of 12 V or 0 V, but connected in parallel they give an e.m.f. of 6 V.

### SAQ 8.6

Apply Kirchhoff's laws to the circuit shown in *figure 8.10* to deduce the values of current that will be shown by the ammeters $A_1$, $A_2$ and $A_3$.

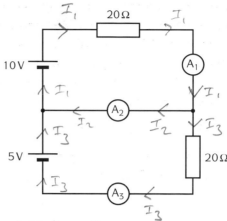

● **Figure 8.10** Kirchhoff's laws make it possible to deduce the ammeter readings.

## Resistor combinations

You are already familiar with the formulae used to calculate the combined resistance $R_{total}$ of two or more resistors connected in series or in parallel. To derive these formulae we have to make use of Kirchhoff's laws. (These derivations follow the same principles as the corresponding derivations for capacitor combinations in chapter 7.)

### Resistors in series

For two resistors connected in series (*figure 8.11*), the current flowing through each resistor is the same. (Current is conserved – Kirchhoff's first law.) The p.d. *V* across the combination is equal to the sum of the p.d.s across the two resistors:

$$V = V_1 + V_2$$

Since $V = IR_{total}$, $V_1 = IR_1$ and $V_2 = IR_2$, we can write:

$$IR_{total} = IR_1 + IR_2$$

Cancelling the common factor of *I* gives:

$$R_{total} = R_1 + R_2$$

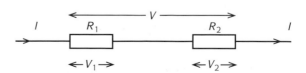

● **Figure 8.11** Resistors in series.

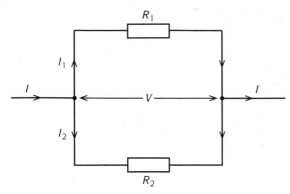

● *Figure 8.12* Resistors connected in parallel.

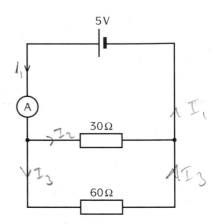

● *Figure 8.13*

## Resistors in parallel

For two resistors connected in parallel *(figure 8.12)*, we have a situation where the current flowing divides between them. Hence, using Kirchhoff's first law, we can write:

$$I = I_1 + I_2$$

If we apply Kirchhoff's second law to the loop that contains the two resistors, we have:

$$I_1R_1 - I_2R_2 = 0\,V$$

(because there is no source of e.m.f. in the loop). This equation says that the two resistors have the same p.d. *V* across them. Hence we can write:

$$I = \frac{V}{R_{\text{total}}} \qquad I_1 = \frac{V}{R_1} \qquad I_2 = \frac{V}{R_2}$$

Substituting in $I = I_1 + I_2$ and cancelling the common factor *V* gives:

$$\frac{1}{R_{\text{total}}} = \frac{1}{R_1} + \frac{1}{R_2}$$

### SAQ 8.7

There are two ways to calculate the current *I* flowing through the ammeter in *figure 8.13*. Both should give the same answer.

**a**  Apply Kirchhoff's laws to deduce *I*.

**b**  Calculate the combined resistance $R_{\text{total}}$ of the two parallel resistors, and hence deduce *I*.

## Potential dividers

A potential divider is part of a circuit used to produce a small voltage from a larger one (see *Basic Physics 1 and 2*, chapter 5). The larger voltage *V* is connected across two resistors in series, and the sum of the p.d.s across these two must then equal *V*. *Figure 8.14* shows one such arrangement. The voltmeter measures the p.d. $V_B$ across $R_B$.

In this circuit, $R_A$ is smaller than $R_B$, so it has a smaller share of the applied p.d. *V*. Provided the current flowing to the voltmeter is small, we have:

$$V_B = \frac{VR_B}{(R_A + R_B)}$$

Substituting in the values gives:

$$V_B = \frac{6\,V \times 400\,\Omega}{(200\,\Omega + 400\,\Omega)} = 4\,V$$

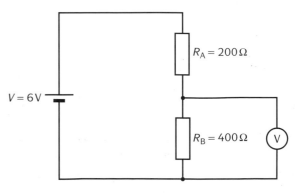

● *Figure 8.14*  A potential divider circuit.

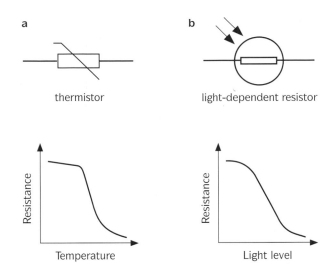

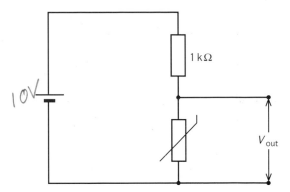

**a**

thermistor

**b**

light-dependent resistor

Resistance

Temperature

Resistance

Light level

● *Figure 8.15* Two components with variable resistances: **a** a thermistor's resistance changes with temperature; **b** a light-dependent resistor's resistance depends on the level of illumination.

## *Thermistors and LDRs*

If a thermistor is used in place of one of the resistors, the potential divider can provide a potential difference which depends on the temperature. (A thermistor is a type of resistor with a resistance that changes rapidly as the temperature changes – see *figure 8.15a*.)

Similarly, a light-dependent resistor can be used in a potential divider to give a potential difference which depends on the level of illumination. (An LDR is a resistor with a resistance that decreases as the light level increases – see *figure 8.15b*.)

### SAQ 8.8 _____

A thermistor is used in the circuit shown in *figure 8.16*. Its resistance changes from $20 \text{k}\Omega$ at $20\,°\text{C}$ to $100\,\Omega$ at $60\,°\text{C}$. Calculate $V_{out}$ at these two temperatures.

### SAQ 8.9 _____

The thermistor in the circuit of *figure 8.16* is replaced with an LDR. Explain whether $V_{out}$ will increase or decrease when a bright light is shone on to the LDR.

● *Figure 8.16* A thermistor incorporated in a potential divider circuit.

## Voltage–temperature characteristics

A thermistor can act as the sensor for an electronic system that responds to temperature changes. Such a system might operate, for example, a fire alarm when the temperature rises too high. It might control the temperature in an incubator in a maternity ward where premature babies are cared for.

To design such a system, the thermistor must be incorporated as part of a potential divider. Then it is necessary to know how the voltage output depends on the temperature. You can investigate the voltage–temperature characteristics of such a circuit using a datalogger *(figure 8.17)*. The temperature probe of the datalogger records the temperature of the water bath, and the second

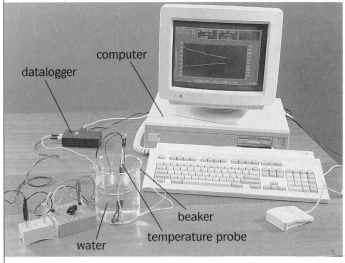

● *Figure 8.17* Using a datalogger to investigate the characteristics of a thermistor.

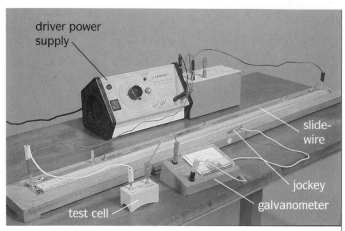

driver power supply

slide-wire

jockey

galvanometer

test cell

● *Figure 8.18* A slide-wire potentiometer, used for comparing potential differences.

input to the datalogger records the voltage output of the potential divider. The temperature can be raised rapidly by pouring amounts of boiling water into the water bath. The datalogger then records both temperature and voltage, and the computer gives a display of the voltage against temperature.

Note that there are two general types of thermistor: negative temperature coefficient (NTC), with a resistance that falls as the temperature rises, and positive temperature coefficient (PTC), with a resistance that rises sharply as the temperature rises.

## *Potentiometers*

A potentiometer is a device based on the principle of a potential divider. It is used to compare potential differences. A slide-wire form of potentiometer is shown in *figure 8.18*; the slide-wire is a 1 m length of resistance wire mounted on a board with a metre rule alongside. A circuit diagram is shown in *figure 8.19*.

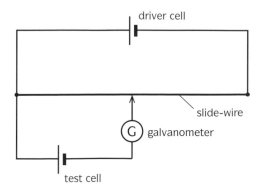

driver cell

slide-wire

G galvanometer

test cell

● *Figure 8.19* Circuit diagram for a potentiometer.

By looking at how a potentiometer is set up, we can see the way it is used to compare two potential differences. First, a driver supply, such as a 2 V accumulator or a power supply with low internal resistance, is connected across the ends of the slide-wire. The positive terminal is connected to the left-hand end of the wire, so that a steady current flows through the wire from left to right.

Now, suppose we want to investigate the e.m.f. of a second cell, the test cell. The positive terminal of this cell is also connected to the left-hand end of the slide-wire. The negative terminal is connected via a sensitive centre-zero galvanometer to a jockey, a metal device for making contact with the slide wire. The jockey is touched on to the slide-wire. The galvanometer needle will deflect, showing that a current is flowing through the test cell. The jockey is touched on to the slide-wire at different points, until a position is found where there is no deflection of the galvanometer needle. At this point, the potentiometer is said to be balanced.

## Explaining the potentiometer

Before we consider practical ways in which a potentiometer can be used, we will look at how Kirchhoff's laws can explain what is happening when the balance point has been reached.

*Figure 8.20a* shows the potentiometer when balanced. A current $I$ flows through the slide-wire, 'pushed' by the driver cell. The length of wire, measured from the left-hand end, has resistance $R$. So the p.d. across this length is simply $IR$. If we apply Kirchhoff's second law to the lower loop, we have:

$$\mathcal{E} = IR$$

If the circuit is unbalanced, as shown in *figure 8.20b*, then a small current $i$ flows from the test cell, and we have:

$$\mathcal{E} = (I - i)R$$

We can only achieve balance ($i$ becomes zero) with the correct value of $R$, which occurs with the correct length of resistance wire. If the jockey is touched on to the slide-wire to one side of the balance point, the current $i$ flows one way, and the

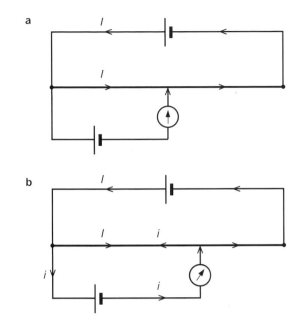

● **Figure 8.20** A potentiometer circuit:
**a** in a balanced condition;
**b** unbalanced.

needle deflects to one side; with the jockey on the other side of the balance point, *i* flows the other way and the needle deflects the other way.

The potentiometer is a kind of potential divider because the jockey divides the slide-wire into two sections, giving the desired p.d. to balance **ℰ**.

The great value of a potentiometer is that, at the balance point, no current flows from the test cell. It can therefore be used to find the e.m.f. of the cell; there are no 'lost volts'. Because a balanced potentiometer draws no current from the cell under investigation, it can be thought of as a voltmeter of infinite resistance. This is to be compared with a moving-coil voltmeter (with a resistance of about $10\,k\Omega$) or a digital voltmeter (resistance $1\,M\Omega$).

Note that it is essential that the slide-wire is uniform along its length. It must have constant resistance per unit length so that, when a steady current flows through it, the p.d. across any length of the wire is proportional to the length.

### SAQ 8.10

If the driver cell of a potentiometer provides a p.d. of 2.0 V across the slide-wire, and the test cell has an e.m.f. of 1.5 V, where will the balance point be?

## Practical uses

In principle, a potentiometer can only be used to compare potential differences. Here are two important ways in which this comparison of potential differences is useful.

1 Comparing the e.m.f.s of two cells *(figure 8.21)*. The length $l_1$ of the slide-wire at the balance point for cell 1 is found, then the corresponding length $l_2$ for cell 2 is found. The ratio of their e.m.f.s is then simply given by:

$$\frac{\mathcal{E}_1}{\mathcal{E}_2} = \frac{l_1}{l_2}$$

If one cell is a standard cell with an e.m.f. that is known to a high degree of precision, the e.m.f. of the other cell can then be calculated.

2 Comparing two resistors *(figure 8.22)*. A circuit is set up with the two resistors in series, so that they have the same current flowing through them. The p.d.s across the two resistors are connected in turn to the potentiometer. The p.d. across $R_1$ gives a balance point $l_1$; the p.d. across $R_2$ gives a balance point $l_2$. Since they have the same current flowing through them, their p.d.s are proportional to their resistances, and we have:

$$\frac{R_1}{R_2} = \frac{l_1}{l_2}$$

If the value of one of the resistances is known accurately, the other can be calculated.

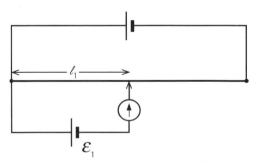

● **Figure 8.21** A potentiometer circuit for comparing the e.m.f.s of two cells. To find $l_2$, the cell $\mathcal{E}_1$ is replaced by cell $\mathcal{E}_2$.

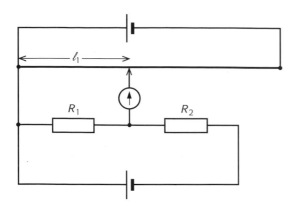

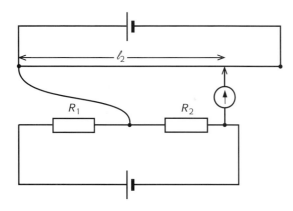

● **Figure 8.22** A potentiometer circuit for comparing two resistors.

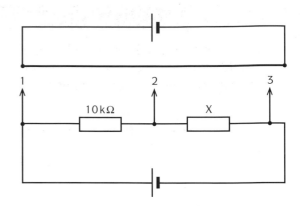

● *Figure 8.23*

## SAQ 8.11

A student sets up the circuit shown in *figure 8.23* using a standard $10\,k\Omega$ resistor to find the resistance of the resistor X. First, he connects leads 1 and 2 into the potentiometer circuit, and finds a balance length of 58 cm. Next, he incorrectly connects leads 1 and 3 into the circuit, and finds a balance length of 85 cm.

**a** What is the resistance of X?

**b** Where would the balance point be with leads 2 and 3 correctly used to find X?

## Potentiometer points

There are several practical points worth noting when using a slide-wire potentiometer.

■ The driver cell must provide a steady voltage, otherwise the p.d. along the slide-wire will vary, and the balance point will not be consistent.

■ The slide-wire must be uniform, otherwise there will not be a uniform change in potential along its length.

■ The jockey should be touched gently on to the slide-wire, and not scraped along it, otherwise the wire could be damaged and become non-uniform.

■ The galvanometer should be sensitive, otherwise an accurate balance point cannot be found.

■ Ideally, the balance point should be towards the right-hand end of the slide-wire, so that the error in measuring the length $l$ is small.

## SUMMARY

■ Kirchhoff's first law represents conservation of current at a point in a circuit.

■ Kirchhoff's second law states that the sum of all the e.m.f.s around a circuit loop is equal to the sum of all the p.d.s around that circuit loop. This follows from the conservation of energy.

■ Kirchhoff's laws can be used to deduce the formulae for the combined resistance of resistors in series and in parallel.

■ Thermistors and light-dependent resistors can be used in potential divider circuits to provide p.d.s that are dependent on temperature and light level respectively.

■ A slide-wire potentiometer is used to compare potential differences. In practice, it can be used to determine the e.m.f. of a cell, and to compare resistors.

## Questions

1 Use Kirchhoff's second law to deduce the p.d. across *R* in the circuit shown in *figure 8.24*, and hence deduce the value of *R*.

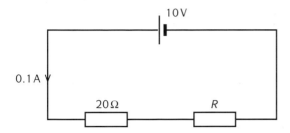

● **Figure 8.24**  Circuit for question 1.

2 Apply Kirchhoff's laws to find the current flowing at point X in the circuit shown in *figure 8.25*. In which direction is the current flowing?

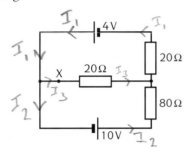

● **Figure 8.25**  Circuit for question 2.

3 A potential divider circuit is required which will give an output voltage that increases as the temperature increases. A thermistor is to be used with a resistance that decreases as the temperature increases. Draw a suitable circuit for the potential divider, showing the connections for the output voltage.

4 The results of an experiment to determine the e.m.f. $\mathcal{E}$ of a cell (using a circuit like that shown in *figure 8.21*) are shown below. Use them to determine $\mathcal{E}$.

    balance length with
        standard Weston cell      = 44.9 cm
    balance length with test cell   = 78.9 cm
    e.m.f. of standard Weston cell  = 1.0183 V

# Alternating current 1

● **Figure 9.1** Electric street lighting first came into use in the 1880s. This photograph was taken in Manchester in 1914.

Nowadays this has been standardised across much of Europe, and we have an alternating supply described as '230 V, 50 Hz'.

In this chapter we will look at some of the reasons why a.c. has been chosen as standard. First, however, we must take a close look at the nature of alternating current.

## Sinusoidal current

An alternating current can be represented by a graph such as that shown in *figure 9.2*. This shows that the current varies cyclically. During half of the cycle, the current is positive, and in the other half it is negative. This means that the current flows

## Describing alternating current

Mains electricity in the UK is a supply of alternating current (a.c.). Mains electricity first became generally available towards the end of the nineteenth century (*figure 9.1*); at that time a great number of different voltages and frequencies were used in different parts of the country. In some places, the supply was direct current (d.c.).

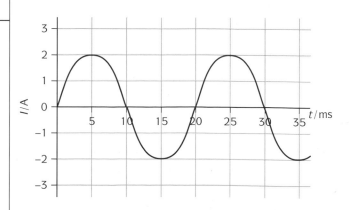

● **Figure 9.2** A sinusoidal alternating current.

alternately one way and then the other in the wires in which it is travelling. Whenever you use a mains appliance, current flows backwards and forwards in the wires between you and the power station where it is being generated. At any instant in time, the current has a particular magnitude and direction given by the graph.

The graph has the same shape as the graphs used to represent simple harmonic motion (see chapter 3), and it can be interpreted in the same way. The electrons in a wire carrying a.c. thus move back and forth with s.h.m.

● *Figure 9.3* Generators in the generating hall of a large power station.

## SAQ 9.1

The following questions relate to the graph of *figure 9.2*:

**a** What is the value of the current $I$ when $t = 5\,\text{ms}$? In which direction is it flowing?

**b** At what time does the current next have the same value, but negative?

**c** What is the time $T$ for one cycle?

**d** What is the frequency of the alternating current?

## An equation for a.c.

As well as drawing a graph, we can write an equation to represent alternating current. This equation tells us the value of the current $I$ at any time $t$:

$$I = I_0 \sin(\omega t)$$

where $\omega$ is the angular frequency of the supply, measured in $\text{rad s}^{-1}$. This is related to the frequency $f$ in the same way as for s.h.m:

$$\omega = 2\pi f$$

The quantity $I_0$ is known as the **peak value** of the alternating current, found from the highest point on the graph.

## SAQ 9.2

**a** What are the values of $I_0$ and $\omega$ for the alternating current represented by the graph of *figure 9.2*?

**b** Write an equation to represent this current.

## SAQ 9.3

An alternating current (measured in amperes, A) is represented by the equation:

$$I = 5 \sin(120\pi t)\,\text{A}$$

**a** What are the values for this current of $I_0$, $\omega$ and $f$? What is the period $T$ of the oscillation?

**b** Sketch a graph to represent the current.

## Alternating voltages

Alternating current is produced in power stations by large generators like those shown in *figure 9.3*. In principle, a generator consists of a coil rotating in a magnetic field. An e.m.f. is induced in the coil according to the laws of electromagnetic induction. You should not be surprised after studying chapter 3 that, for a coil rotating with uniform circular motion in a uniform magnetic field, the induced e.m.f. varies sinusoidally. There is a close relationship between circular motion and s.h.m.

Because the voltage $V$ varies sinusoidally, we can write an equation to represent it which has the same form as the equation for alternating current:

$$V = V_0 \sin(\omega t)$$

where $V_0$ is the peak value of the voltage. We can also represent this graphically, as shown in *figure 9.4*.

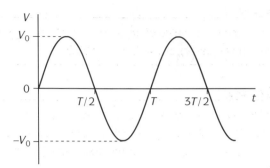

● **Figure 9.4** An alternating voltage.

## SAQ 9.4

An alternating voltage (in V) is represented by the equation:

$$V = 300 \sin(100\pi t)\,V$$

(If you use the formula, remember that $100\pi t$ is in radians when you calculate the sine value.)

**a** What are the values of $V_0$, $\omega$ and $f$ for this voltage?

**b** What is the value of $V$ when $t = 0.002\,s$?

**c** Sketch a graph to show two complete cycles of this voltage.

# Power and a.c.

We use mains electricity to supply us with energy. If the current and voltage are varying all the time, doesn't this mean that the power is varying all the time too? The answer to this is yes, it is. You may have noticed that a fluorescent lamp flickers continuously, especially if you observe it out of the corner of your eye. A tungsten filament lamp would flicker too, but the frequency of the mains has been chosen so that the filament does not have time to cool down noticeably between peaks in the supply.

### Investigating flicker

If you connect a low-voltage filament lamp to a low frequency supply from a signal generator, you can see it flicker as it heats up and cools down because the current through it varies.

Investigate the effect of varying the frequency. At what frequency does the flickering disappear? Is the flicker more noticeable out of the corner of your eye?

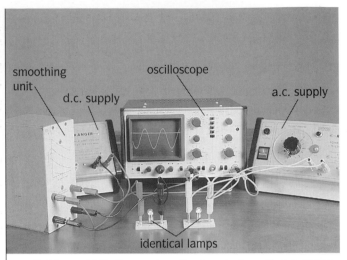

● **Figure 9.5** Comparing direct and alternating currents that supply the same power. The lamps are equally bright.

## Comparing a.c. and d.c.

Because the power supplied by an alternating current is varying all the time, we need to have some way of describing the average power which it is supplying. To do this, we compare an alternating current with a direct current, and try to find the direct current that supplies the same average power as the alternating current.

*Figure 9.5* shows how this can be done in practice. Two lamps are placed side-by-side; one is connected to an a.c. supply, and the other to a d.c. supply (which is smoothed to ensure that it is perfectly steady). The two power supplies are adjusted so that the lamps are equally bright, and their output voltages are compared on the double-beam oscilloscope.

A typical trace is shown in *figure 9.6*. This shows that the a.c. trace sometimes rises above the d.c.

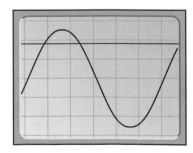

● **Figure 9.6** The oscilloscope trace from the experiment shown in *figure 9.5*.

trace, and sometimes falls below it. This makes sense: sometimes the a.c. is delivering more power than the d.c., and sometimes less, but the average power is the same for both.

There is a mathematical relationship between the d.c. voltage and the peak value $V_0$ of the alternating voltage. The d.c. voltage is about 70% of $V_0$. (You might have expected it to be about half, but it is more than this, because of the shape of the sine graph.) This steady d.c. voltage is known as the **root-mean-square** (r.m.s.) value of the alternating voltage. In the same way, we can think of the root-mean-square value of an alternating current, $I_{rms}$:

The root-mean-square value of an alternating current is that steady direct current which delivers the same average power as the a.c. to a resistive load.

(The lamps in the experiment above are the 'resistive loads'.) A full analysis shows that $I_{rms}$ is related to $I_0$ by:

$$I_{rms} = \frac{I_0}{\sqrt{2}} \quad \text{or} \quad I_{rms} \simeq 0.707 \times I_0$$

This is where the factor of 70% comes from. Note that this factor only applies to sinusoidal alternating currents.

### SAQ 9.5

What is the r.m.s. value of an alternating current represented (in amperes) by $I = 2.5 \sin(100\pi t)$?

### SAQ 9.6

The UK mains supply to domestic users has an r.m.s. voltage $V_{rms}$ of 230 V. (Note that it is the r.m.s. value which is generally quoted, not the peak value.) What is the peak value of the supply?

## Calculating power

When an alternating voltage is connected across a resistor, it makes an alternating current flow through it. To calculate the average power dissipated in the resistor, we can use the usual formulae for power:

$$P = I^2 R = IV = \frac{V^2}{R}$$

Remember that it is essential to use the r.m.s. values of $I$ and $V$. If you use peak values, your answer will be too great by a factor of 2.

We shall now do an example. What is the average power dissipated when a sinusoidal p.d. of peak value 25 V is connected across a 20 Ω resistor?

---

### R.m.s.

The importance of r.m.s. values is that they allow us to apply equations from our study of direct current to situations where the current is alternating. We will now briefly consider the origin of the term root-mean-square.

You should recall that the power $P$ dissipated by a current $I$ flowing through a resistance $R$ is given by:

$P = I^2 R$

Thus the power is proportional to the square of the current. *Figure 9.7* shows how we can calculate $I^2$ for an alternating current. The current $I$ varies sinusoidally, and during half of each cycle it is negative. However, $I^2$ is always positive (because the square of a negative number is positive). Notice that $I^2$ varies up and down, and that it has twice the frequency of the current. Now, if we consider $<I^2>$, the average (mean) value of $I^2$, we find that its value is half the peak value (because the graph is symmetrical). To find the r.m.s. value of $I$, we now take the square root of $<I^2>$. This introduces a factor of the square root of a half, or $1/\sqrt{2}$.

Summarising this process: to find the r.m.s. value of the current, we find the root of the mean of the square of the current – hence r.m.s.

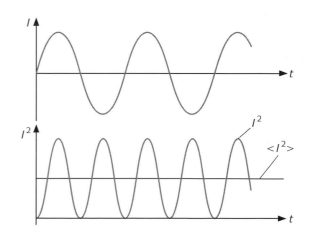

● *Figure 9.7* A.c. is alternately positive and negative; $I^2$ is always positive.

First, we must calculate the r.m.s. value of the p.d.:

$$V_{rms} = \frac{V_0}{\sqrt{2}} = \frac{25\,V}{\sqrt{2}} = 17.7\,V$$

Now we can calculate the average power dissipated:

$$P = \frac{V^2}{R} = \frac{(17.7\,V)^2}{20\,\Omega} = 15.6\,W$$

(If we had used $V_0$ rather than $V_{rms}$, we would have found $P = V^2/R = (25\,V)^2/20\,\Omega = 31.3\,W$, which is twice the correct answer.)

### SAQ 9.7

What is the average power dissipated when a sinusoidal alternating current, with a peak value of 3.0 A, flows through a 100 Ω resistor?

### SAQ 9.8

A sinusoidal voltage of peak value 325 V is connected across a 1 kΩ resistor.

**a** What is the r.m.s. value of this voltage?

**b** Use $V = IR$ to calculate the r.m.s. current which flows through the resistor.

**c** What is the average power dissipated in the resistor?

# Why use a.c. for electricity supply?

There are several reasons for preferring alternating voltages for a national electricity supply system. The most important reason is that a.c. can be transformed to high voltages for transmission, so that the current flowing is reduced, and this leads to lower power losses in the transmission lines.

The UK is served by the National Grid (*figure 9.8*), which transmits electrical power along thousands of kilometres of high-voltage power lines from the power stations to the millions of consumers. Typically, the generators at a power station produce electrical power at a voltage of 25 kV. This is transformed up to a voltage which may be as high as 400 kV. (Transformers are discussed in detail in the next section.) This high voltage brings problems: the lines must be

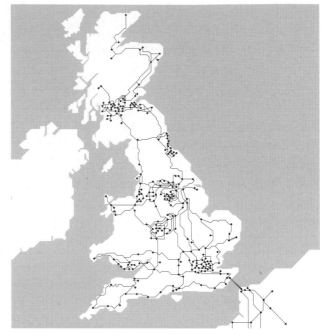

● *Figure 9.8* The UK National Grid distributes power around the country at high voltages.

suspended high above the ground between pylons, and high-quality insulators are needed to prevent current passing from the cables to the pylons (*figure 9.9*). The power must then be transformed back to a lower voltage to make it safe and manageable for the user.

## *Investigating power losses*

As current flows through transmission lines (wires), it loses power because of the resistance of the lines. The wires become warm; this is known as resistive heating or ohmic heating. You can see the effect of

● *Figure 9.9* Power lines are often suspended from insulators on the arms of pylons.

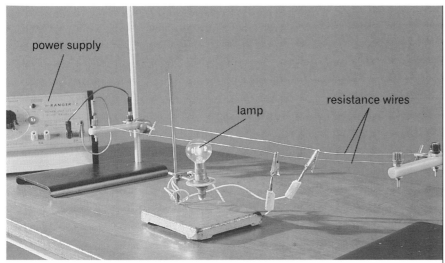

● *Figure 9.10* A model of power lines.

this using the arrangement shown in *figure 9.10*. Here, the 12 V power supply represents a power station, and the resistance wires represent the transmission lines. A 12 V lamp is connected between the wires close to the supply; it glows brightly. There is little resistance in the circuit between the supply and the lamp. Now the lamp is connected further from the supply, and it is found to be dimmer. The current has to flow through a greater length of resistance wire, so there is more resistance in the circuit. The current is smaller, and the p.d. across the lamp is smaller. Power has been wasted in the transmission lines.

## Calculating power losses

When power is transmitted at a higher voltage, a smaller current is required. Since the power dissipated is given by $P = I^2R$, it follows that the smaller the current, the smaller is the wastage of power. It is simplest to see this using a numerical example.

A power company has the choice of transmitting power at 50 kV and 200 A, or at 250 kV and 40 A. The transmission lines have a resistance of 10 Ω. Note that the power transmitted in both cases is the same, since $P = VI$, and 50 kV × 200 A = 250 kV × 40 A = 10 MW.

Now we can calculate the power lost in the lines in each case. For $I = 200$ A, we have:

$$P = I^2R = (200\,\text{A})^2 \times 10\,\Omega = 400\,\text{kW}$$

For $I = 40$ A, we have:

$$P = (40\,\text{A})^2 \times 10\,\Omega = 16\,\text{kW}.$$

So decreasing the current by a factor of 5 reduces the power wasted by a factor of 25. (Note that, in the first case, 4% of the power transmitted is wasted.)

*SAQ 9.9*

Power of 1 MW is transmitted at a p.d. of 100 kV along power lines with a resistance of 5 Ω.

a   Calculate the current which flows in the power lines.

b   Calculate the power wasted by resistive heating of the lines.

c   How much power would be wasted if the same power were transmitted at a p.d. of 500 kV?

## *Economic savings*

The resistive heating of power lines is a waste of money, in two ways. First, it costs money to generate power because of the fuel needed. Second, more power stations are required, and power stations are expensive. The use of transformers to transform power to high voltages for transmission saves a few percent of the national bill for electrical power, and means that fewer expensive power stations are needed.

High-voltage transmission over long distances also means that it is possible to have relatively few, very large power stations spread around the country. It is claimed that this gives economies of scale, though this is debated by some environmentalists who would like to see many small, local power stations.

## Transformers

To change the voltage of an alternating power supply, a transformer is used. *Figure 9.11* shows the construction of a simple transformer. The primary coil of $N_p$ turns of wire is wound around the

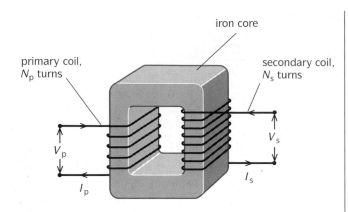

● **Figure 9.11** Defining quantities for a simple iron-cored transformer.

iron core. The secondary coil of $N_s$ turns is wound on the opposite side of the core. (Many different configurations are possible, with different shapes of core, and with the coils wound separately or one on top of the other. The arrangement in this illustration shows clearly the relationship between the coils and the core.)

The p.d. $V_p$ across the primary coil causes an alternating current $I_p$ to flow. This produces an alternating magnetic field in the soft iron core. The secondary coil is thus in a changing magnetic field, and an alternating current $I_s$ is induced in it. (The laws of electromagnetic induction are discussed in chapter 11 of *Basic Physics 1 and 2*.) There is thus an alternating p.d. $V_s$ across the secondary coil.

Note that there is no electrical connection between the primary coil and the secondary coil. Energy is transferred from one to the other via the magnetic field in the core.

A transformer cannot work with direct current. Alternating current is needed to produce a changing magnetic field, which can induce an e.m.f. in the secondary coil. This answers our earlier question: alternating currents are needed for electricity supply so that transformers can be used. These transformers are used to step up to (and step down from) high voltages, which reduce the resistive losses in transmission lines.

## Transformer relationships

If there is no power lost in a transformer, it follows that the quantity $I \times V$ is the same for both primary (p) and secondary (s) coils:

$$I_p V_p = I_s V_s \quad \text{or} \quad \frac{V_p}{V_s} = \frac{I_s}{I_p}$$

There is a second relationship which relates the p.d.s across the coils to the number of turns in each coil:

$$\frac{N_p}{N_s} = \frac{V_p}{V_s}$$

In other words, the ratio of the voltages is equal to the ratio of the numbers of turns. A transformer thus changes the voltage by a factor equal to its 'turns-ratio'. (In these equations, voltages and currents are taken to be either all peak values or all r.m.s. values. Don't mix the two.)

The transformer in *figure 9.12a* is known as a **step-up transformer**. The secondary p.d. $V_s$ is three times the primary p.d. $V_p$, because there are three times as many turns on the secondary as on the primary. It increases the p.d. by a factor of three.

a

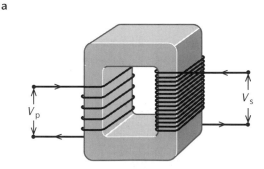

b

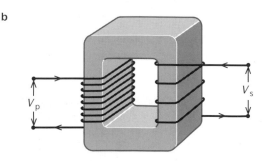

● **Figure 9.12** Two transformers: **a** step-up and **b** step-down.

The transformer in *figure 9.12b* is a step-down transformer, because there are fewer secondary turns than primary turns.

If we look at the step-up transformer shown in *figure 9.12a*, we can understand how it steps up the p.d. according to $N_p/N_s = V_p/V_s$. The current flowing through the five turns of the primary coil produces a varying magnetic field in the core. The flux density depends on both the primary p.d. and the number of turns $N_p$. The magnetic flux also passes through the secondary coil, where it induces an e.m.f. This is $V_s$, which is proportional to the number of turns on the secondary coil $N_s$. Hence the induced e.m.f. depends on $N_s$ and the flux density, which in turn depends on $N_p$ and the primary p.d. $V_p$.

Note that a step-up transformer increases the p.d., but the current in the secondary coil must be reduced by the same factor (because the total amount of power cannot increase).

Note also that the relationships quoted above assume that no power is lost in the transformer. In practice, some power is lost because of the resistance of the transformer coil windings; some power is also lost as the magnetic flux in the core flows back and forth. The windings and the core tend to become warm. Large transformers such as those shown in *figure 9.13* handle a large amount of power. A small percentage is wasted, and the resulting heat is carried away by cooling fluid pumped around the transformer and through the fins which are visible in the photograph.

To minimise the losses in the core, a soft magnetic material must be used; that is, one in which magnetic flux can flow back and forth easily. The direction of magnetisation must be easily reversed. Soft iron is a suitable material, and in commercial transformers, iron is usually alloyed with a small fraction of silicon. (The opposite of a soft magnetic material is a hard magnetic material. Steel is a hard magnetic material, and is used for making permanent magnets because it retains its magnetisation.)

Other losses occur in the core due to **eddy currents**. The core is an electrically conducting material, and it is in a changing magnetic field. Consequently, induced eddy currents flow in it at right angles to the magnetic flux, and energy is dissipated in the core because of its electrical resistance. To reduce this problem, the core is usually made of thin sheets (laminae); the flux can flow easily through the length of the sheets, but the eddy currents cannot flow readily from one sheet to the next.

● *Figure 9.13* These large transformers at a power station require elaborate cooling systems to remove heat produced in the windings and core.

## SAQ 9.10

**a** What is the turns-ratio of the transformer shown in *figure 9.12b*?

**b** If an alternating p.d. of peak value 10 V is connected across its primary coil, what will be the induced e.m.f. across its secondary coil? (Assume that there are no power losses in the transformer.)

## SAQ 9.11

*Table 9.1* shows information about three transformers. Copy and complete the table. (Assume no power losses in the transformers.)

| Transformer | $N_p$ | $N_s$ | $V_p/V$ | $V_s/V$ | $I_p/A$ | $I_s/A$ | $P/W$ |
|---|---|---|---|---|---|---|---|
| A | 100 | 500 | 230 | | 1.0 | | |
| B | 500 | 100 | 230 | | 1.0 | | |
| C | 100 | | 12 | 240 | 0.2 | | |

● *Table 9.1* Details of three transformers

# Rectification

Many electrical appliances work with alternating current. For example, an electrical heater will work equally well with d.c. or a.c. Many electric motors are designed to work with a.c., and they usually rotate at a rate equal to the a.c. frequency (or a multiple of it). However, there are many appliances such as electronic equipment which require d.c. How can this be supplied when the mains gives an alternating voltage?

The answer is that the alternating mains must be rectified. **Rectification** is the name for the process of changing an alternating current into a direct current.

A simple way to do this is to use a diode, which is a component that will only allow current to flow in one direction. *Figure 9.14* shows a circuit for doing this, together with a graph to show the effect. You will see that the output voltage is always positive, but that it does go up and down. This is still technically direct current, because the current only flows in one direction.

This type of rectification is known as **half-wave** rectification. For half of the time the voltage is zero, and this means that the power available from a half-wave rectified supply is reduced.

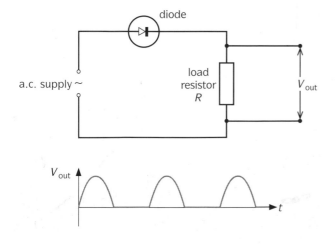

● **Figure 9.14** Half-wave rectification of a.c.

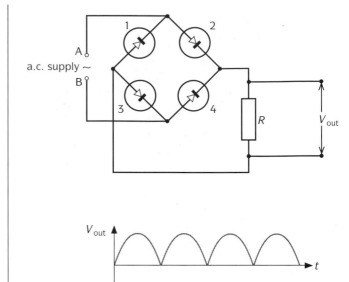

● **Figure 9.15** Full-wave rectification of a.c. using a diode bridge.

## The bridge rectifier

To overcome this problem of reduced power, a bridge rectifier circuit is used. This consists of four diodes connected across the alternating voltage, as shown in *figure 9.15*. The resulting output voltage across the load resistor *R* is **full-wave** rectified.

The way in which this works is shown in *figure 9.16*. During the first half of the a.c. cycle, terminal A is positive. Current flows through diode 2, downwards through *R* and through diode 3 to terminal B. In this half of the cycle, the current flows through diode 2 rather than diode 1, which is pointing the wrong way. During the second half of the cycle, terminal B is positive. Current flows through diode 4, downwards through *R* and through diode 1 to terminal A. Note that in both halves of the cycle, current flows the same way through *R*. In *figure 9.16* the current flows downwards through *R*, and so the top end of *R* must be positive.

A bridge rectifier can be constructed using light-emitting diodes (LEDs). These light up when current flows through them. By connecting such a bridge to a slow a.c. supply (for instance 1 Hz from a signal generator), you can see the sequence in which the diodes conduct during rectification.

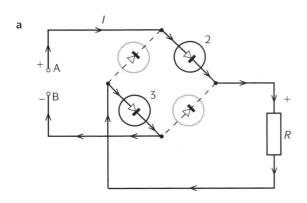

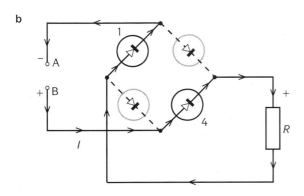

● **Figure 9.16** Current flow during full-wave rectification.

## SAQ 9.12

Explain why, when terminal B in *figure 9.16* is positive (during the second half of the cycle), the current flows through diodes 1 and 4, but not through diodes 2 and 3.

## *Smoothing*

In order to produce steady d.c. from the 'bumpy' d.c. that results from rectification, a smoothing capacitor must be incorporated in the circuit. This is shown in *figure 9.17*. The idea is that the capacitor charges up and maintains the voltage at a high level. It discharges gradually when the rectified voltage drops, but the voltage soon rises again and the capacitor charges up again. A small capacitor discharges more rapidly than a large capacitor, and this gives rise to greater ripple on the output voltage. Similarly, if the load resistor is small, the capacitor discharges rapidly. In practice, the greater the value of the quantity $R \times C$, the smoother the rectified a.c.

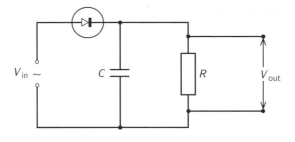

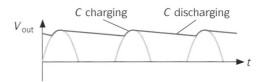

● **Figure 9.17** A smoothing capacitor is connected across (in parallel with) the load resistor.

## Power supplies

You can investigate the output voltage of a power supply using an oscilloscope *(figure 9.18)*. You may be surprised to find that many laboratory power supplies give an unsmoothed output.

Smoothing units are available which consist of a large capacitor in a box with terminals. You can investigate the effect of one of these on the output voltage of an unsmoothed d.c. power supply.

Note that the a.c. voltages shown on the front panel of a power supply are usually r.m.s. values. Similarly, a.c. voltmeters and ammeters give r.m.s. readings.

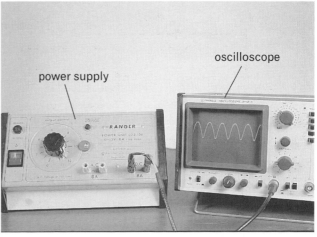

● **Figure 9.18** Investigating the d.c. output of a power supply – it is not as steady as you might expect!

## SAQ 9.13

Sketch the following voltage patterns:

**a**  a sinusoidal alternating voltage;

**b**  the same voltage as **a**, but half-wave rectified;

**c**  the same voltage as **b**, but smoothed;

**d**  the same voltage as **a**, but full-wave rectified;

**e**  the same voltage as **d**, but smoothed.

## SUMMARY

■ Alternating electrical supplies are usually sinusoidal. An alternating current can be represented by $I = I_0 \sin(\omega t)$, where $I_0$ is the peak value of the current.

■ The average power dissipated in a resistive load by an alternating current is half the peak power; this leads to the definition of root-mean-square current. For a sinusoidal a.c., $I_{rms} = I_0/\sqrt{2}$.

■ To reduce losses in transmission lines, electrical power is usually transmitted at high voltages. This allows the current to be reduced, and so resistive losses are less.

■ Transformers are used to change the voltage. Voltage is stepped up or down in proportion to the turns ratio of the transformer.

■ To convert a.c. to d.c., diodes are used. A single diode gives half-wave rectification. A bridge of four diodes gives full-wave rectification. A capacitor smooths the rectified voltage by storing charge.

## Questions

1  In the USA, the mains frequency is 60 Hz. Write an equation to represent a sinusoidal current of frequency 60 Hz and r.m.s. value 2.0 A.

2  A step-up transformer has a turns ratio of 10 : 1. When an alternating p.d. of 20 V is connected across the primary coil, a current of 50 mA flows in it.
   **a**  Calculate the values of the p.d. across the secondary coil and the current flowing in it.
   **b**  In practice, the secondary p.d. is found to be 180 V and the secondary current is 4.5 mA. What percentage of the power is wasted in the transformer?

3  An amplifier supplies 30 W of power to a loudspeaker at a p.d. of 12 V. The leads to the loudspeaker have a resistance of 0.1 Ω. Calculate the power wasted in the leads.

4  A student wires a bridge rectifier circuit incorrectly as shown in *figure 9.19*. Explain what you would expect to observe when an oscilloscope is connected across the load resistor *R*.

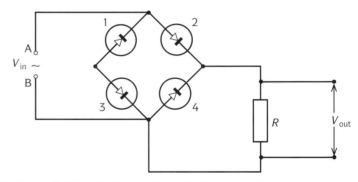

● *Figure 9.19*  A bridge rectifier circuit that is wired incorrectly.

5  A bridge rectifier circuit is used to rectify an alternating current through a resistor *R*. A smoothing capacitor *C* is connected across *R*. *Figure 9.20* shows how the current varies. What changes would you expect:
   **a**  if *R* was increased;
   **b**  if *C* was decreased?

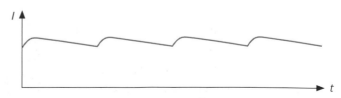

● *Figure 9.20*  A smoothed, rectified current.

# *Alternating current 2*

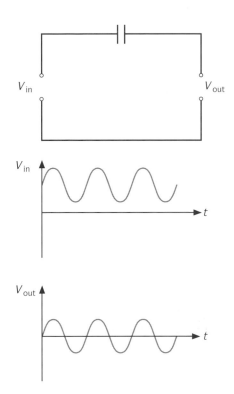

● **Figure 10.1**  A capacitor connected in series removes any d.c. from an alternating current.

## Capacitors and a.c.

Capacitors have many uses in a.c. circuits. In the last chapter, we saw how they are used to smooth rectified current. They are also used to remove any direct current that may have been added to an alternating current, as shown in *figure 10.1*. Here, the capacitor is used because it will not allow direct current to flow through it. The resulting current is pure sinusoidal a.c.

A capacitor will not permit the flow of direct current because it represents a break in the circuit. So how does it allow a.c. to flow through it? The answer is that, as the voltage rises, the capacitor charges up. One plate becomes positively charged, and this repels positive charge from the opposite plate. In effect, positive charge has passed through the capacitor.

The circuit shown in *figure 10.2* can be used to investigate how a.c. passes through a capacitor.

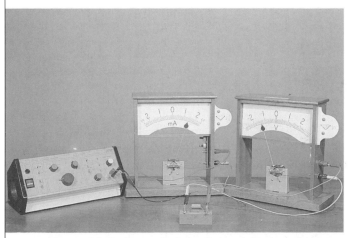

● **Figure 10.2**  A practical circuit for observing phase differences in an a.c. circuit with a capacitor.

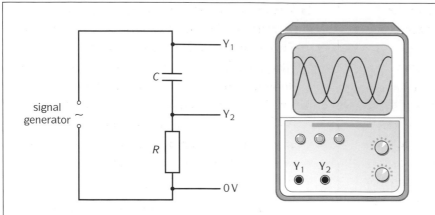

● **Figure 10.3** A circuit for observing phase differences using an oscilloscope.

The circuit in *figure 10.2* includes a voltmeter connected across the capacitor to show the p.d. *V* across it. In addition, there is an ammeter in the circuit to show the current *I* flowing. The supply is a signal generator capable of providing a low frequency (of about 1 Hz) voltage. Moving-coil meters are used because they allow you to see how *I* and *V* are varying. In this experiment, the two meters are seen to oscillate at the same frequency, which is determined by the frequency of the supply. The surprising thing is that the two meters oscillate out of step with one another. The current reaches its maximum value and starts to fall before the p.d. reaches its maximum value.

This can be shown using a double-beam oscilloscope *(figure 10.3)*. A resistor is added to the circuit, in series with the capacitor. The oscilloscope display shows that the current peaks one quarter of a cycle before the p.d. We say that there is a phase difference of quarter of a cycle between *I* and *V*, with *I* leading *V*. However, the voltage across the resistor varies in step with the current. This behaviour is summarised here:

> The current through a capacitor has a phase lead of quarter of a cycle over the alternating p.d. across the capacitor. The current through a resistor varies in phase with the p.d. across it.

**SAQ 10.1** _____

**a** Sketch a pair of graphs to show how *I* and *V* vary over two complete cycles for a capacitor. (Hint: *figure 10.3* will help.)

**b** Sketch a similar pair of graphs for a resistor.

## Explaining phase differences

Why is there this phase difference between the current and the p.d. for a capacitor? We need to think about how the capacitor charges up and discharges as the a.c. flows through it. This is illustrated in *figure 10.4*.

In the first quarter of the cycle, the p.d. is positive and increasing. The capacitor charges up – current flows into it, so *I* is positive.

In the second quarter, the p.d. is still positive but now it is decreasing. The capacitor discharges – current flows out of it. Hence, in this part of the cycle, *V* is positive but *I* is negative.

In the third quarter, the p.d. is negative and becoming more negative. The capacitor charges

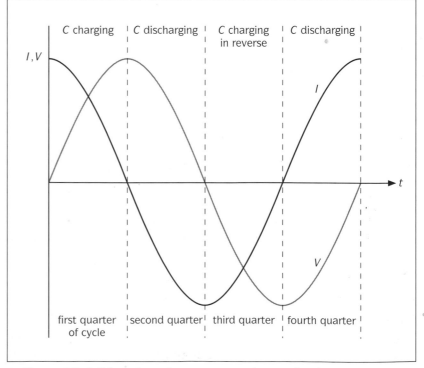

● **Figure 10.4** When the p.d. across a capacitor reaches its maximum value, the current flowing falls to zero.

up, but the opposite way round to earlier in the cycle. $I$ is still negative, but it approaches zero at the point where the capacitor is fully charged.

In the fourth quarter, the p.d. is still negative but is now approaching zero. The capacitor discharges once again. $I$ increases from zero.

Another, more mathematical, way of explaining this is to think about how the charge $Q$ stored by the capacitor varies. Since $Q$ is proportional to $V$ (because $Q = CV$), we can think of the $V$ graph as showing how $Q$ varies. The current $I$ is the rate of change of $Q$, so we can find $I$ from the gradient of the $Q$–$t$ graph. In the first quarter-cycle, $Q$ is increasing but levelling off, so $I$ is positive and decreasing towards zero. In the second quarter-cycle, $Q$ is decreasing more and more rapidly, so $I$ is negative and becoming more negative.

## SAQ 10.2

Continue this explanation to show how $I$ is related to $Q$ in the second half of the cycle.

## SAQ 10.3

Sketch a graph to show how the charge $Q$ stored by a capacitor varies during a complete cycle of a.c. Indicate where the capacitor is charging up, and where it is discharging.

## The reactance of a capacitor

A capacitor will allow an alternating current to flow through it. But how much current passes through? This depends on the reactance $X_C$ of the capacitor. The reactance of a capacitor is analogous to the resistance of a resistor. For a resistor we have $V = IR$, and for a capacitor we have:

$$V = IX_C$$

In this equation, $V$ and $I$ are the peak values of the p.d. and the current. (Note that the ratio of $V$ to $I$ keeps changing as they vary out of step with one another, so we have to specify that the reactance is defined in terms of their peak values.) From this equation you can see that reactance is measured in ohms.

The reactance depends on two things: the capacitance $C$ of the capacitor, and the frequency $f$ of the p.d.

- The greater the capacitance, the greater the current that flows, and so the reactance is less. This is because a big capacitor stores more charge for a given voltage, and so more current flows in and out as the voltage changes.
- The higher the frequency, the greater the current that flows, and again the reactance is less. A capacitor will not allow d.c. ($f = 0\,\text{Hz}$) to pass through; the higher the frequency, the easier it is for current to flow through it.

It turns out that the reactance of a capacitor is given by:

$$X_C = \frac{1}{\omega C}$$

where $\omega = 2\pi f$ is the angular frequency of the a.c. supply. You should be able to see from this equation that a small capacitor at low frequencies has a high reactance, and will tend to impede the flow of current more than a large capacitor at high frequencies.

## SAQ 10.4

Which is greater: **a** the reactance of a $100\,\mu\text{F}$ capacitor to an alternating p.d. of frequency $1\,\text{kHz}$, or **b** the reactance of a $10\,\mu\text{F}$ capacitor at $500\,\text{kHz}$?

## SAQ 10.5

A $1000\,\mu\text{F}$ capacitor is connected to a $2\,\text{V}$, $50\,\text{Hz}$ alternating supply. What current will flow in the circuit?

## Investigating capacitive reactance

To measure the reactance of a capacitor and to investigate how it depends on frequency, you need to measure both the p.d. across it and the current flowing through it. *Figure 10.5* shows a suitable circuit. Voltmeter $V_C$ measures the p.d. across C. The resistor $R$ is included in the circuit so that you can find the current from the value of $R$ and the reading on the second voltmeter $V_R$.

The power supply is a signal generator, so that the frequency can be varied over a range of values. At higher frequencies, the reactance decreases, and a typical graph of reactance against frequency is shown in *figure 10.6*. Note that the larger capacitor has the smaller reactance.

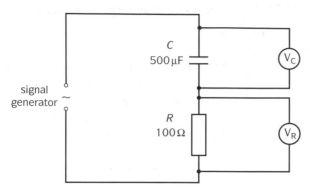

● **Figure 10.5** A circuit for investigating the frequency dependence of capacitive reactance.

## SAQ 10.6

The reactance $X_C$ of a capacitor is inversely proportional to the frequency $f$ of the alternating p.d. across it. Sketch a graph of $X_C$ against $1/f$ to show the results you would expect to find for two capacitors, one of which has twice the capacitance of the other. Indicate which line corresponds to the greater capacitance.

# Inductors and a.c.

An inductor is a coil of wire. Many electrical appliances involve coils of wire – motors, generators and transformers, for example. In addition, coils are sometimes included in circuits for purposes that will become clear in the remainder of this chapter. It is thus important to know how inductors behave in electric circuits where alternating current is flowing.

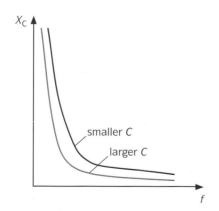

● **Figure 10.6** The frequency dependence of capacitive reactance.

How does a coil behave when a current flows through it? If the current is steady (d.c.) then the coil behaves like an electromagnet. A magnetic field is established in and around the coil.

The story is rather different with a changing current. If the current changes, the magnetic field changes. Now we have a conductor (the coil) in a changing magnetic field. From our study of electro-magnetic induction (see chapters 10 and 11 of *Basic Physics 1 and 2*) we know that this will result in an induced e.m.f. This acts to oppose the change producing it (Lenz's law), and so it tends to stop the current from changing. If the current is increasing, the induced e.m.f. pushes back to make it difficult for the current to grow; if the current is decreasing, the induced e.m.f. reverses and tends to maintain the current and the flux at their previous levels (*figure 10.7*).

A large coil with many turns has a greater inductance $L$ than a small coil with fewer turns. (Inductance is measured in units called henries, H.) This means that it is easier to change the current through an inductor with a low value of $L$ than through one with a high value of $L$.

## *Investigating inductance and a.c.*

You can investigate the behaviour of an inductor connected to an alternating supply in a similar way to the investigation of capacitors shown earlier. In this case, a coil with an iron core is connected to a signal generator (*figure 10.8*). A resistor is also included in the circuit. The oscilloscope traces

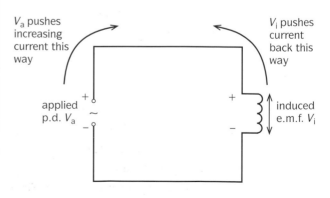

● **Figure 10.7** An inductor opposes changes in current.

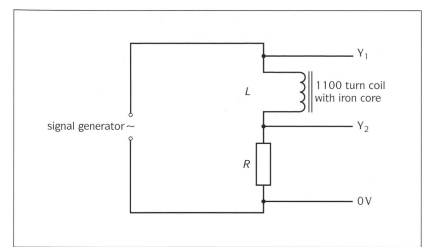

● *Figure 10.8* A circuit for displaying phase differences with an oscilloscope, for an a.c. circuit containing an inductor.

● *Figure 10.9* A mnemonic for remembering phase differences in a.c. circuits.

show the p.d. across *L* and the p.d. across *R*, which shows how the current is varying in the circuit.

This experiment shows the opposite effect to that observed for capacitors. The current through the inductor peaks after the p.d. across it. There is a phase difference of one quarter of a cycle between them. *Figure 10.9* shows a mnemonic which is useful for remembering the phase relationships in a.c. circuits.

## Explaining phase differences

Why does the current through an inductor lag behind the p.d. across it, as shown in *figure 10.10*? We need to consider how these quantities change during a complete cycle.

At the beginning of the first quarter of the cycle, the current is increasing rapidly. The magnetic flux within the coil is therefore changing rapidly (by Faraday's law), and the e.m.f. across the coil is maximum.

At the end of the first quarter, the current has reached its maximum value and is momentarily constant. Since the

flux is not changing, the induced e.m.f. is zero.

### SAQ 10.7

Explain how the current is changing **a** at the end of the second quarter of the cycle, and **b** a quarter of a cycle later still. Explain how this determines the value of the e.m.f. at these points.

## The reactance of an inductor

An inductor will allow direct current ($f = 0\,\text{Hz}$) to pass through unhindered (unless it has resistance as well as inductance). However, it hinders the flow of a.c., and the higher the frequency, the more it is impeded. Similarly, the greater the inductance, the more it impedes the flow of a.c. We can define the reactance $X_L$ of an inductor in a similar way to that of a capacitor:

$$V = IX_L$$

Again, this is analogous with the definition of resistance from $V = IR$, and inductive reactance is measured in ohms. Note, however, that we cannot talk about the resistance of an inductor or a capacitor, because *V* and *I* are not in phase with each other, as they are for a resistor.

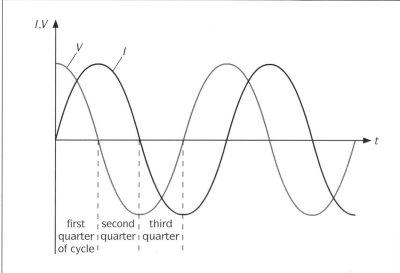

● *Figure 10.10* The p.d. across an inductor reaches its peak value before the current.

The reactance of an inductor depends on its inductance $L$ and the frequency of the a.c. voltage across it. It turns out that $X_L$ is given by:

$$X_L = \omega L$$

This shows clearly that reactance is proportional to both $f$ and $L$.

## SAQ 10.8

Which has the greater reactance: **a** a 10 mH inductor at 200 Hz, or **b** a 100 mH inductor at 50 Hz?

## SAQ 10.9

What current will flow through a 0.05 H inductor when it is connected to a 230 V, 50 Hz a.c. supply?

## Investigating inductive reactance

You can investigate how the reactance of an inductor depends on frequency in a similar way to the investigation of capacitive reactance described earlier. A suitable circuit is shown in *figure 10.11*. The 1 kW resistor allows the current to be calculated; the voltmeter $V_L$ shows the p.d. across the inductor.

Varying the signal generator allows the reactance to be determined at a range of frequencies. In principle, $X_L \propto f$, and a graph of $X_L$ against $f$ should be a straight line. In practice, the coil may have resistance as well as reactance, and this is liable to distort the graph, particularly at low frequencies.

| $f$/Hz | $V_R$/V | $I$/mA | $V_L$/V | $X_L$/$\Omega$ |
|---|---|---|---|---|
| 500 | 2.75 | 2.75 | 1.75 | 636 |
| 1 000 | 2.15 | 2.15 | 2.35 | 1090 |
| 2 000 | 1.9 | | 2.6 | |
| 3 000 | 1.75 | | 2.8 | |
| 4 000 | 1.6 | | 2.9 | |
| 6 000 | 1.5 | | 3.1 | |
| 8 000 | 1.4 | | 3.3 | |
| 10 000 | 1.3 | | 3.4 | |

● **Table 10.1**  Results of an experiment to investigate the reactance of an inductor (note that $R = 1\,k\Omega$)

## SAQ 10.10

**a**  Sketch a graph to show how you would expect the reactance of a coil to depend on the frequency of the a.c. supply across it.

**b**  Add a second line representing the reactance of a coil having twice the inductance of the first.

## SAQ 10.11

*Table 10.1* shows the results for an experiment similar to the one described above. Copy the table, complete it and plot a graph to show how the coil's reactance depends on frequency. Use the graph to estimate the coil's inductance.

# $L$–$C$ circuits

An important effect can be observed when a circuit is constructed with both a capacitor and an inductor, wired together in parallel. The circuit shown in *figure 10.12* includes lamps to show the current that is flowing at different points in the circuit.

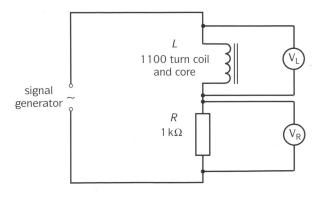

● **Figure 10.11**  A circuit for investigating the frequency dependence of inductive reactance.

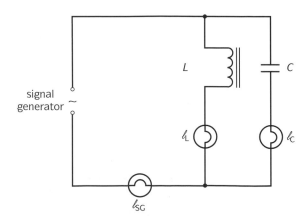

● **Figure 10.12**  A parallel $L$–$C$ circuit.

If the frequency of the signal generator is initially set at a low value, the lamp $\ell_L$ will be brighter than lamp $\ell_C$. As the frequency is increased, $\ell_L$ becomes dimmer while $\ell_C$ becomes brighter.

This tells us that the current flowing through $L$ is decreasing (because the inductive reactance is increasing as the frequency increases) and the current flowing through $C$ is increasing (because the capacitive reactance is decreasing).

## Resonance

The surprising thing is that, at the point where $\ell_L$ and $\ell_C$ are equally bright, the third lamp $\ell_{SG}$ is very dim or completely unlit. This shows that there is apparently no current flowing from the signal generator.

This circuit demonstrates an example of electrical resonance. *Figure 10.13* shows how the reactances of $C$ and $L$ depend on frequency $f$: $X_L$ increases with frequency, while $X_C$ decreases with frequency. At a certain point, the two reactances are equal, and this is when resonance occurs. But how can we have no current flowing from the signal generator but equal currents flowing in $C$ and $L$? To answer this, we need to think about the phases of these currents.

The current through $C$ leads the p.d. by quarter of a cycle; the current through $L$ lags behind the p.d. by the same amount. The two currents are thus half a cycle out of phase with each other. The

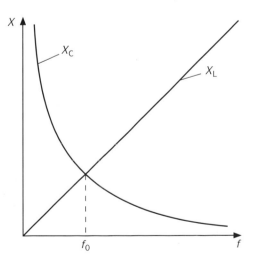

● *Figure 10.13* At the resonant requency, the capacitive and inductive reactances are equal.

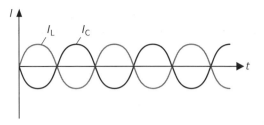

● *Figure 10.14* At resonance, the currents through $L$ and $C$ are equal and opposite.

current from the supply is equal to the sum of these currents. *Figure 10.14* shows that the sum of two equal currents that are exactly out of phase with each other is zero. You can observe this using a double-beam oscilloscope. Replace the lamps $\ell_L$ and $\ell_C$ with resistors that have resistances of a few ohms; connect the two inputs of the oscilloscope across these resistors to see how the two currents vary. The screen shows two traces of equal amplitudes but in antiphase.

So what is going on at resonance? A large current flows back and forth through $L$ and $C$. As the current is flowing one way through the capacitor, it flows the other way through the inductor. The capacitor charges up, using current from the inductor. The capacitor then discharges, so that current flows the other way, back into the inductor. There is a constant flow of current back and forth between $C$ and $L$.

During this cycle, energy is stored alternately in the electric field within the capacitor, and in the magnetic field within the inductor. The energy initially comes from the supply. You should recognise this as being a form of resonance. There is a **resonant frequency** $f_0$ at which it occurs. The system is 'pushed' at this frequency by the signal generator. The current oscillates back and forth at $f_0$. Energy is constantly being exchanged between two forms, electrical and magnetic.

### SAQ 10.12

*Figure 10.15* shows the current $I_L$ through an inductor and the current $I_C$ through a capacitor in a parallel $L$–$C$ circuit. One diagram represents the situation at a frequency below the resonant frequency, the other at a frequency above the resonant frequency. Which is which? How can you tell?

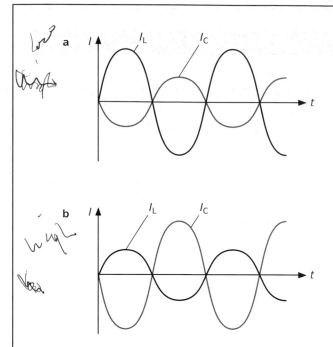

● **Figure 10.15** See *SAQ 10.12.*

## Calculating the resonant frequency

Resonance occurs in a parallel *L–C* circuit when the reactances of the two components are equal:

$$X_L = X_C$$

For the inductor, $X_L = \omega L = 2\pi f L$. For the capacitor, $X_C = 1/\omega C = 1/2\pi f C$. Therefore, at resonance we have:

$$2\pi f_0 L = \frac{1}{2\pi f_0 C}$$

So:

$$f_0 = \frac{1}{2\pi \sqrt{LC}}$$

Hence a parallel circuit containing a 10 mH inductor and a 100 mF capacitor will resonate at a frequency given by:

$$f_0 = \frac{1}{2\pi \times \sqrt{0.01\,\text{H} \times 10^{-4}\,\text{C}}} = \frac{1}{2\pi \times \sqrt{10^{-6}\,\text{s}^2}}$$

$$= 160\,\text{Hz}$$

### SAQ 10.13 _____

A parallel *L–C* circuit includes a 200 pF capacitor and a 50 mH inductor. What is the value of the resonant frequency?

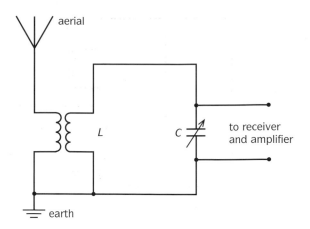

● **Figure 10.16** A tunable circuit for a radio receiver.

## Using L–C circuits

A tuner in a radio set makes use of a parallel *L–C* circuit. This is shown in *figure 10.16*. The signal from the aerial is very weak, and consists of many different frequencies, corresponding to the various broadcasting stations. The tuner must select the desired station and produce a voltage which can then be amplified.

When the dial on the tuner is turned, this alters the variable capacitor. When the resonant frequency of the circuit matches the frequency of the desired station, a large current flows back and forth between *L* and *C*. This produces a relatively large voltage across *C*, which can then be passed to the amplifier.

### SAQ 10.14 _____

A parallel *L–C* circuit like that shown in *figure 10.16* is required to resonate at 100 MHz. This will be part of an FM (VHF) radio tuner. An inductor is available with an inductance of $5 \times 10^{-8}$ H. What value of capacitor is required?

## Resistive damping

As in any resonant system, electrical oscillations can be damped. Energy must be removed from the system, and this is achieved by including a resistor in the circuit. (In practice, all inductors have resistance, so there will always be some damping.)

The circuit shown in *figure 10.17* can be used to investigate the effect of damping. With a low value

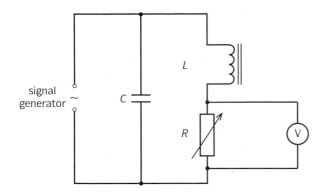

● **Figure 10.17** A circuit for investigating the effect of resistive damping on resonance.

of $R$, the voltage across $R$ increases rapidly when the frequency is close to the resonant frequency $f_0$. With greater resistance, there is a smaller increase in the voltage, showing that the current has been damped by the resistance. *Figure 10.18* shows how the voltage across $R$ changes as the frequency is changed through resonance, for different degrees of damping. This shows the same pattern as is observed for damped mechanical oscillations.

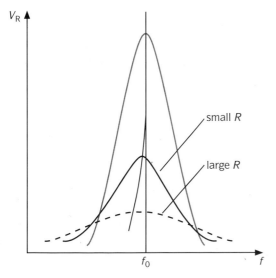

● **Figure 10.18** The effect of resistive damping on resonance. Note that the resonant frequency drops slightly as the resistance is increased.

## SUMMARY

■ A capacitor permits a.c. to flow through it. The higher the frequency of the a.c., the greater the current which flows (for a given voltage); its reactance decreases as the frequency increases according to the equation $X_C = 1/\omega C$. The current through a capacitor leads the voltage by quarter of a cycle.

■ An inductor will also allow a.c. to flow. The higher the frequency of the a.c., the smaller the current which flows because an inductor is a component that opposes changes in current; its reactance increases as the frequency increases, according to the equation $X_L = \omega L$. The current through an inductor lags behind the voltage by quarter of a cycle.

■ Resonance occurs in a parallel $L-C$ circuit when the reactances of the capacitor and the inductor are equal. This occurs at a frequency $f_0$, given by:

$$f_0 = \frac{1}{2\pi\sqrt{LC}}$$

The resonance is damped by resistance in the circuit.

## Questions

1  An inductor is described as 'a circuit component that opposes changes in current'. Explain why this is a consequence of Lenz's law of electromagnetic induction.

2  A capacitor will not permit a steady direct current to flow through it. Explain how an alternating current can flow through a capacitor.

3  **a** Calculate the reactances of a 10 mH inductor and a 500 pF capacitor at a frequency of 1 kHz.
    **b** If these two components were connected in a parallel circuit, what would be its resonant frequency?

4  What value of capacitance has the same reactance as a 250 mH inductor at a frequency of 50 Hz?

5  What is the phase difference in radians between the current and the p.d. in an a.c. circuit containing only **a** a resistor, **b** a capacitor or **c** an inductor?

# Answers to self-assessment questions

The answers are sometimes given to more figures than are allowed by the data, to allow for checking.

## Chapter 1

**1.1** a 30° b 180°, 105°

**1.2** a 0.52 rad, 1.57 rad, 1.83 rad
b 28.6°, 43.0°, 180°, 90°
c $\pi/3$ rad, $\pi/2$ rad, $\pi$ rad, $2\pi$ rad

**1.3** 1.67 rad

**1.4** a 0.017 rad b $2.58 \times 10^6$ km

**1.5** 0.105 rad s$^{-1}$, $1.75 \times 10^{-3}$ rad s$^{-1}$, $1.45 \times 10^{-4}$ rad s$^{-1}$

**1.6** a $7.3 \times 10^{-5}$ rad s$^{-1}$ b 465 m s$^{-1}$

**1.7** $v = 2\pi \times 200\,\text{m}/30\,\text{s} = 42\,\text{m s}^{-1}$
$a = v^2/r = (41.9\,\text{m s}^{-1})^2/200\,\text{m} = 8.8\,\text{m s}^{-2}$

**1.8** a $2.66 \times 10^{-6}$ rad s$^{-1}$
b $2.72 \times 10^{-3}$ m s$^{-2}$
c $2.0 \times 10^{20}$ N

**1.9** Tension in string must have a vertical component to balance the weight of the conker.

**1.10** In level flight, lift balances the weight. During banking, the vertical component of lift is less than the weight, so the aeroplane loses height unless lift can be increased.

**1.11** 23.1 km

### End-of-chapter questions

**1** 0.26 rad hr$^{-1}$

**2** a 25.1 rad s$^{-1}$ b 7.5 m s$^{-1}$
c 189 m s$^{-2}$ d 18.9 N

**3** 4870 N

**4** a $2.5 \times 10^{-6}$ rad s$^{-1}$
b $2.5 \times 10^6$ s (= 29.1 days)

**5** The normal reaction (contact force) of the wall of the slide has a horizontal component, which provides the centripetal force. If you are going fast, you need a bigger force, so the horizontal component must be greater. This happens when you move up the curve of the wall of the slide.

## Chapter 2

**2.1** 7.8 km s$^{-1}$

**2.2** The satellite will gradually slow down (its kinetic energy will decrease) and spiral down towards the Earth's surface. Small thruster rockets are normally used to give the satellite an occasional push to maintain its speed and height above the Earth.

**2.3** 20 600 km

### Box questions on Jupiter's moons

**A** Plot a graph of $T^2$ against $r^3$, and use the gradient, as in the text.
Mass of Jupiter = $1.9 \times 10^{27}$ kg

**B** $1.8 \times 10^8$ m

### End-of-chapter questions

**1** $GMm/r^2 = mv^2/r$; cancelling and substituting $r = d/2$ gives the required result.

**2** a Observation of cloud, temperature and pressure.
b Looking for likely rock formations.
c Reports are transmitted direct to a geostationary satellite from difficult locations.

**3** Mass of Mars = $6.4 \times 10^{23}$ kg

**4** a $2.2 \times 10^6$ m s$^{-1}$, $1.5 \times 10^{-16}$ s
b Speed would decrease; period would increase.

# Chapter 3

**3.1** The mass is the weight on the end of the pendulum. The central position is where the mass is hanging vertically downwards. The restoring force is the force of gravity. (In fact, it is the component of the mass's weight at right angles to the string.)

**3.2** **a** 2.0 cm **b** 0.40 s
**c** 31 cm s$^{-1}$ **d** 0.50 m s$^{-2}$

**3.3** At the extreme left of the oscillation, the acceleration is positive (towards the right).

**3.4** Gradient = 0, so $v = 0$ m s$^{-1}$.

**3.5** **a** 0 cm s$^{-1}$ **b** 47 cm s$^{-1}$ **c** 0 cm s$^{-2}$

**3.6** **a** 0.5 s **b** 2 Hz **c** $4\pi$ rad s$^{-1}$

**3.7** **a** Gravitational potential energy.
**b** Gravitational potential energy has changed to kinetic energy by the midpoint of the oscillation; then kinetic energy changes back to gravitational potential energy again.

**3.8** See *figure*.

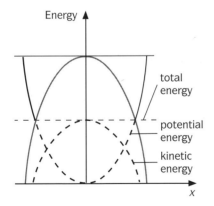

● *Answer for* SAQ 3.8

## End-of-chapter questions

**1** They are not in equilibrium at the midpoint of their 'oscillation'; the force on them does not vary uniformly. When they are in the air, the force (gravity) is constant.

**2** **a** See *figure*.

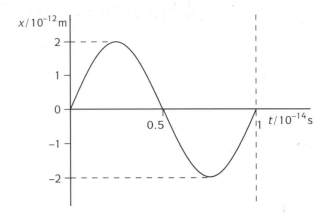

● *Answer for* question 2a

**b** Use the gradient at the steepest point;
$v_{max} = 1.3 \times 10^3$ m s$^{-1}$

**3** **a** 2 s **b** 0.5 Hz **c** $\pi$ rad s$^{-1}$

**4** **a** 0.37 m s$^{-1}$ **b** 0.137 J **c** 0.137 J
**d** 1.86 m s$^{-2}$ **e** 3.72 N

# Chapter 4

**4.1** At point D there is a dark fringe, because rays 1 and 2 differ in path length by one-and-a-half wavelengths ($3\lambda/2$). At point E there is a bright fringe, because the path difference is $2\lambda$.

**4.2** Double the distance gives double the fringe separation: $x = 2.8$ mm.

**4.3** **a** $x = \lambda D/a$, so decreasing $a$ increases $x$.
**b** Blue light consists of shorter wavelengths, so $x$ is less.
**c** For larger $D$, $x$ is greater, so there is greater precision in $x$.

**4.4** $D$ and $a$ are fixed, so $\lambda_1/x_1 = \lambda_2/x_2$, and so $x_2 = 450$ nm $\times$ 2.4 mm/600 nm = 1.8 mm. (Or, wavelength is 3/4 of previous value, so spacing of fringes is 3/4 of previous value.)

**4.5** **a** $S_1C = 2.000\,000\,562$ m;
$S_2C = 2.000\,000\,062$ m
**b** difference = 500 nm

**4.6** For the second-order maximum, rays from adjacent slits have a path difference of $2\lambda$, so they are in phase.

**4.7** **a** 20.4°

**b** Maxima at 31.5°, 44.2°, 60.6°. You cannot have $\sin\theta > 1$. There are 11 maxima.

**4.8** **a** $\theta$ increases, so the maxima are more spread out and there may be fewer of them. **b** $d$ decreases, so again $\theta$ increases.

**4.9** $\theta_{red} = 20.5°$, $\theta_{violet} = 11.5°$, so angular separation $= 9.0°$.

**4.10** The third-order maximum for violet light is deflected through a smaller angle than the second-order maximum for red light.

**4.11** $\dfrac{\sin\theta_1}{\lambda_1} = \dfrac{\sin\theta_2}{\lambda_2}$, so $\sin\theta_2$

$$= \frac{\sin 25° \times 589\,\text{nm}}{656\,\text{nm}}$$

$= 0.379$; hence $\theta_2 = 22.3°$.

## End-of-chapter questions

**1** 3.5 mm

**2** For $n = 2$, $\sin\theta = 0.93$; for $n = 3$, $\sin\theta > 1$.

For $\lambda = 400\,\text{nm}$, $\sin\theta = 1$ gives $n = 3.75$, so 3 is the highest order.

**3** **a** $10x = 8.7\,\text{mm}$
**b** $\theta = 19.12°$
**c** Recalculating part **a** with $10x = 8.8\,\text{mm}$ gives $\lambda = 550\,\text{nm}$; recalculating part **b** with $\theta = 19.22°$ gives $\lambda = 548.7\,\text{nm}$, which is closer to 546 nm. Hence the diffraction grating method is slightly more precise. (In practice, it is much more precise because the fringes are better defined.)

## Chapter 5

**5.1** Any experiment in which a current in a wire or coil produces a magnetic field or in which a magnet is moved near a wire or coil to produce a current or voltage. These experiments are discussed in chapters 8–11 of *Basic Physics 1 and 2*.

**5.2** All waves show reflection, refraction, diffraction and interference. Transverse waves also show polarisation, as discussed later in the chapter.

**5.3** $\varepsilon_0 = 8.8542 \times 10^{-12}\,\text{F m}^{-1}$; most calculators can only give the answer correct to 4 or 5 decimal places.

**5.4** **a** $4.3 \times 10^{14}\,\text{Hz}$ **b** 467 nm, $4.3 \times 10^{14}\,\text{Hz}$ (unchanged)

**5.5** See *table*.

| Radiation | Wavelength range/m | Frequency range/Hz |
|---|---|---|
| radio waves | $>10^6$ to $10^{-1}$ | $< 3 \times 10^9$ |
| microwaves | $10^{-1}$ to $10^{-3}$ | $3 \times 10^9$ to $3 \times 10^{11}$ |
| infrared | $10^{-3}$ to $7 \times 10^{-7}$ | $3 \times 10^{11}$ to $4.3 \times 10^{14}$ |
| visible | $7 \times 10^{-7}$ to $4 \times 10^{-7}$ | $4.3 \times 10^{14}$ to $7.5 \times 10^{14}$ |
| ultraviolet | $4 \times 10^{-7}$ to $10^{-8}$ | $7.5 \times 10^{14}$ to $3 \times 10^{16}$ |
| X-rays | $10^{-8}$ to $10^{-13}$ | $3 \times 10^{16}$ to $3 \times 10^{21}$ |
| $\gamma$-rays | $10^{-10}$ to $10^{-16}$ | $3 \times 10^{18}$ to $3 \times 10^{24}$ |

**5.6** **a** visible light **b** ultraviolet
**c** three **d** 1–100 mm
**e** 400–700 nm **f** $4.3 \times 10^{14}$ to $7.5 \times 10^{14}\,\text{Hz}$

**5.7** The length of the aerial is comparable to a quarter of the wavelength of the longest VHF and UHF television waves. The wavelengths used in other wavebands are much greater than the length of the aerial (hundreds or thousands of metres), so it does not help to receive them.

**5.8** **a** The area is four times as great.
**b** The intensity is a quarter of previous value, so amplitude must be halved.

**5.9** **a** Red light.
**b** The ratio of the intensities is 10 000 : 1, so the ratio of the amplitudes is 100 : 1.

## End-of-chapter questions

**1** Radio waves, microwaves, infrared, visible light, ultraviolet, X-rays or $\gamma$-rays.

**2** Radio waves, microwaves, visible light, X-rays.

**3** The spacing of the planes of atoms in quartz is comparable to the wavelengths of X-rays. The planes act as if they are slits of a diffraction grating.

4    See *figure*.

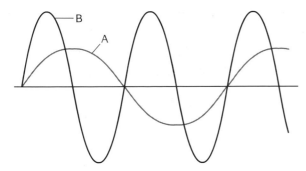

● **Answer for** question 4

# Chapter 6

**6.1**  Charged rods of the same material repel one another (except for ebonite). Unlike rods may attract and repel. We can conclude that glass and Perspex have one type of charge, and polythene and ebonite have the opposite type. The result for two ebonite rods is inconsistent and must be ignored.

**6.2**  a Like charges and like poles repel, so the rule is the same.
b Like charges repel, but like (parallel) currents attract, so the rule is different.

**6.3**  See *figure*.

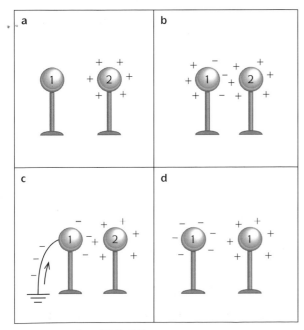

● **Answer for** SAQ 6.3

**6.4**  1 and 2 are initially uncharged. Object 3 attracts electrons from 1 on to 2, leaving 1 with a positive charge. When they are separated, 1 and 2 retain their opposite charges. (This must be done before 3 is removed.)

**6.5**  a One approach is to measure the time taken for the gold leaf to drop between two positions on the scale. For rods having identical dimensions, the ratio of the times will be the ratio of their resistivities.
b The leaf will drop faster, and this will suggest that the rod is a better conductor than it really is. The effect will be more serious for rods having high resistivity.

**6.6**  In crop-spraying, an opposite charge is induced on the ground and the plant.

**6.7**  a A large voltage is established between the nozzle and the object to be sprayed. Charged droplets are attracted to the object and strike it from all sides.
b Paint droplets land on the back as well as the front.
c All of the paint is attracted to the object. Little is wasted on the surroundings.

**6.8**  When the sailors walk on the deck, there is friction between their feet and the deck, which can cause a build-up of electrostatic charge. If the shoes have conducting soles, the charge will not accumulate, but will return to the deck.

**6.9**  Humans are not good conductors, although we are good enough conductors for an electric current to flow when we get an electric shock. (This is because we contain a large amount of water with dissolved salts.) However, neither are we good insulators. To keep us charged up, we must be insulated from the Earth – which is most easily achieved by wearing plastic shoes.

## End-of-chapter questions

1   **a, b** A and B have like charges, but A and C have unlike charges.

c B and C must have unlike charges, so they will attract one another.

2   **a** Free electrons contribute to both electrical and thermal conduction.

**b** A good electrical insulator has very few free electrons. However, it may be a good thermal conductor because heat can conduct via the mechanism of atomic (lattice) vibrations. (See *Basic Physics 1 and 2*, pages 132–4.)

3   **a** The ruler becomes charged by friction. It induces a redistribution of charge in the water, and the water is attracted to the ruler. (Water molecules are polar.)

**b** A metal ruler is a good electrical conductor, so it will not retain its charge.

4   Suppose the comb becomes negatively charged – it has gained electrons in the process of being rubbed by the cloth. Electrons in the paper are repelled by the charged comb, leaving a positive charge close to the comb. This is attracted by the comb, and the paper sticks to the comb.

Now electrons from the comb gradually move onto the paper, which gains an overall negative charge, like the comb. The comb and paper repel one another.

## Chapter 7

7.1   **a** $200\,\mu F$    **b** $4000\,\mu C$

7.2   $2000\,\mu C, 5000\,\mu C, 7000\,\mu C$

7.3   Two $20\,\mu F$ and one $10\,\mu F$ connected in parallel.

7.4   $100\,\mu F$

7.5   **a** $C_{total}$ = one-half (or one-third) of $C$ for two (or three) capacitors.
**b** For $n$ capacitors in parallel, $C_{total} = n \times C$.

7.6   **a** $1/G_{total} = 1/G_1 + 1/G_2$
**b** $G_{total} = G_1 + G_2$

7.7   **a** $33.3\,\mu F$    **b** $300\,\mu F$
**c** $66.7\,\mu F$    **d** $150\,\mu F$

7.8   **a** Four in parallel.
**b** Four in series.
**c** Two in series with two in parallel.

7.9   gradient $= V/Q = 1/C$

7.10  **a** See *table*.

| Q/mC | V/V | Area of strip $\Delta W$/mJ | Sum of areas W/mJ |
|---|---|---|---|
| 1 | 1 | 0.5 | 0.5 |
| 2 | 2 | 1.5 | 2.0 |
| 3 | 3 | 2.5 | 4.5 |
| 4 | 4 | 3.5 | 8.0 |

**b** The graph is a parabola.
**c** $1\,mF$.

7.11  **a** $25\,\mu F$   **b** $4000\,\mu C$
**c** $160\,V$   **d** $80\,mJ$

7.12  See *figure*.

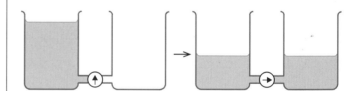

● *Answer for* SAQ 7.12

**a** Half original level.
**b** Halving of energy stored when equal capacitors are connected together.

## End-of-chapter questions

1   Greatest: in parallel, $900\,pF$; least: in series, $60\,pF$.

2   $4\,\mu F$

3   **a** $40\,\mu F$    **b** $0.4\,C$    **c** $2\,kJ$

4   **a** $1.8\,C, 8.1\,J$    **b** $810\,W$
**c** $180\,A$    **d** $0.025\,\Omega$

# Chapter 8

**8.1** 4.5 A

**8.2** 1.5 A, towards P

**8.3** **a** Loop containing two 5 V cells (because only one current is involved).
**b** 1 A

**8.4** 18 Ω

**8.5** In series, the 1 C charge passes through both cells and gains or loses 6 J in each. If they are connected back-to-front, it gains energy in one cell but loses it in the next. In parallel, half the charge flows through each cell, so total energy gained is 6 J.

**8.6** 0.5 A, 0.25 A, 0.25 A

**8.7** **a** 0.25 A   **b** 20 Ω, 0.25 A

**8.8** 9.5 V, 0.91 V

**8.9** Resistance decreases so $V_{out}$ decreases.

**8.10** 75 cm from left-hand end.

**8.11** **a** 4.7 kΩ        **b** 27 cm from left-hand end.

## End-of-chapter questions

**1** 8 V, 80 Ω

**2** 33 mA; this current flows to the right through point X.

**3** See *figure*.

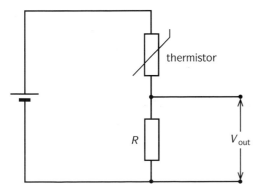

● **Answer for** question 3

**4** 1.79 V

# Chapter 9

**9.1** **a** 2 A, positive      **b** 15 ms
      **c** 20 ms              **d** 50 Hz

**9.2** **a** 2 A, 100π rad s$^{-1}$   **b** $I = 2 \sin(100\pi t)$

**9.3** **a** 5 A, 120π rad s$^{-1}$, 60 Hz, 17 ms
      **b** See *figure*.

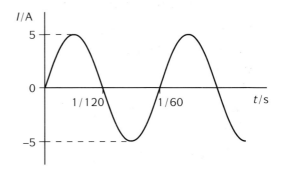

● **Answer for**  SAQ 9.3b

**9.4** **a** 300 V, 100π rad s$^{-1}$, 50 Hz
      **b** 176 V
      **c** See *figure*.

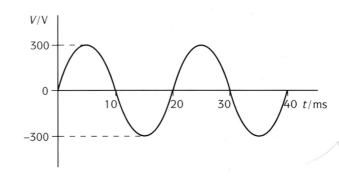

● **Answer for**  SAQ 9.4c

**9.5** 1.8 A

**9.6** 325 V

**9.7** 450 W

**9.8** **a** 230 V      **b** 0.23 A      **c** 53 W

**9.9** **a** 10 A      **b** 500 W      **c** 20 W

**9.10** **a** $N_p : N_s = 2:1$    **b** 5 V (peak value)

**9.11** See *table*.

| Transformer | $N_p$ | $N_s$ | $V_p/V$ | $V_s/V$ | $I_p/A$ | $I_s/A$ | $P/W$ |
|---|---|---|---|---|---|---|---|
| A | 100 | 500 | 230 | 1150 | 1.0 | 0.2 | 230 |
| B | 500 | 100 | 230 | 46 | 1.0 | 5.0 | 230 |
| C | 100 | 2000 | 12 | 240 | 0.2 | 0.01 | 2.4 |

**9.12** Diode 3 is pointing the wrong way, so the current flows through diode 4, through *R* and then through diode 1.

**9.13** See *figure*.

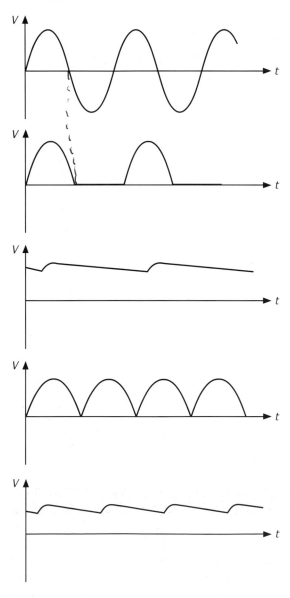

● *Answer for* SAQ 9.13

## End-of-chapter questions

1   $I = 2.83 \sin(120\pi t)$

2   **a** 200 V, 5 mA      **b** 19%

3   0.625 W

4   The voltage will be half-wave rectified. Current can flow through diode 2 when terminal A is positive; when terminal B is positive, current cannot flow because there is no complete path to terminal A.

5   **a** Less pronounced ripple.
    **b** More pronounced ripple.

## Chapter 10

**10.1 a, b**  See *figure*; note that in **b**, the two curves have been drawn with different heights to show clearly that they are in phase with one another; this does not mean that *V* is less than *I*. (A voltage cannot be more or less than a current: they are completely different quantities.)

**a**
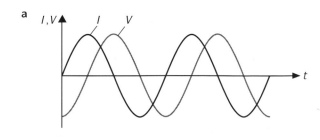

**b**
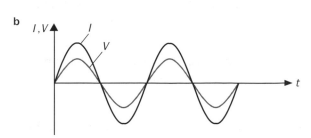

● *Answer for* SAQ 10.1

**10.2** In the third quarter-cycle, $Q$ is becoming increasingly negative. $I$ is negative but decreasing towards zero. In the fourth quarter-cycle, $Q$ is decreasing towards zero at an increasing rate. $I$ is thus positive and increasing, but it levels off to a large, positive value by the end of the cycle.

**10.3** See *figure*.

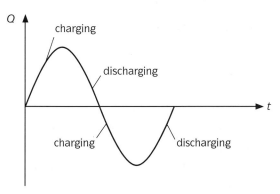

● **Answer for** SAQ 10.3

**10.4 a** (100 μF at 1 kHz) is greater.

**10.5** 0.63 A

**10.6** See *figure*.

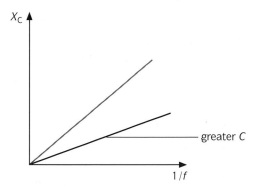

● **Answer for** SAQ 10.6

**10.7 a** The current has dropped to zero and is changing rapidly. The induced e.m.f. therefore is at its maximum value.
**b** The current has reached its maximum value in the reverse direction and is momentarily constant. The induced e.m.f. is therefore zero.

**10.8 b** (100 mH at 50 Hz) has greater reactance.

**10.9** 15 A

**10.10 a, b** See *figure*.

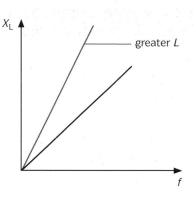

● **Answer for** SAQ 10.10

**10.11** See *table* and *figure*.

Gradient of line at high frequency = $0.136\ \Omega\,\mathrm{Hz}^{-1}$;

$L \simeq 0.136/2\pi = 0.02\,\mathrm{H}$.

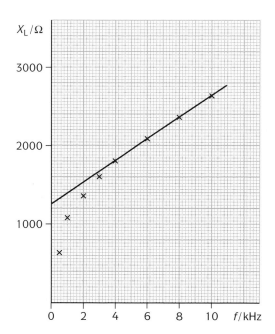

● **Answer for** SAQ 10.11

| $f$/Hz | $V_R$/V | $I$/mA | $V_L$/V | $X_L$/$\Omega$ |
|---|---|---|---|---|
| 500 | 2.75 | 2.75 | 1.75 | 636 |
| 1 000 | 2.15 | 2.15 | 2.35 | 1090 |
| 2 000 | 1.9 | 1.9 | 2.6 | 1370 |
| 3 000 | 1.75 | 1.75 | 2.8 | 1600 |
| 4 000 | 1.6 | 1.6 | 2.9 | 1810 |
| 6 000 | 1.5 | 1.5 | 3.1 | 2070 |
| 8 000 | 1.4 | 1.4 | 3.3 | 2360 |
| 10 000 | 1.3 | 1.3 | 3.4 | 2620 |

**10.12 a** is at a frequency below the resonant frequency $f_0$, because the inductor is allowing more current to flow than the capacitor. **b** is at a frequency above $f_0$, because the capacitor is allowing more current to flow than the inductor.

**10.13** 1.6 MHz

**10.14** 50 pF

## End-of-chapter questions

1      See text on page 74.

2      See text on page 71.

3      **a** 62.8 Ω, 318 kΩ      **b** 71.2 kHz

4      $40.5 \times 10^{-3}$ F

5      **a** 0 (in phase)      **b** $\pi/2$ rad (*I* leads *V*)
       **c** $\pi/2$ rad (*V* leads *I*)

# Index (Numbers in italics refer to figures.)